K·I·D·S
K·I·T·C·H·E·N

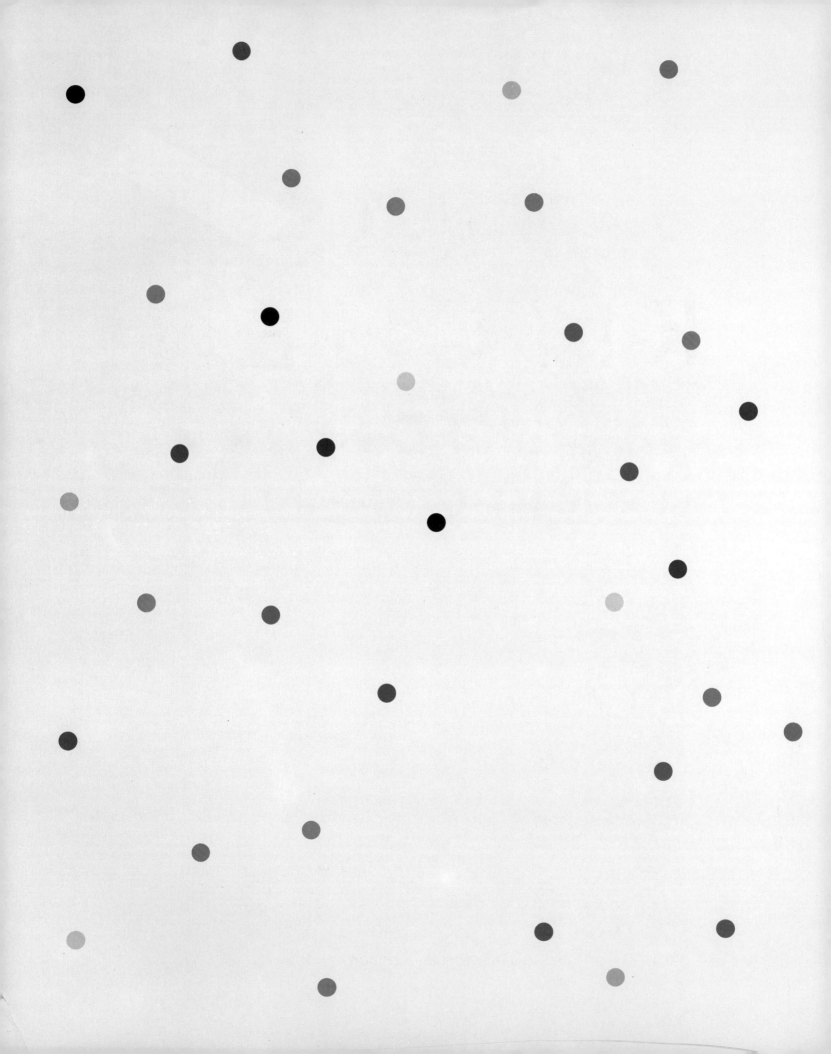

K·I·D·S
K·I·T·C·H·E·N

100 amazing recipes your children can really make

JENNIFER LOW

PHOTOGRAPHY BY MARK BURSTYN

Grub Street • London

This edition produced in 2007 for The Book People
by Grub Street
4 Rainham Close
London SW11 6SS

www.grubstreet.co.uk
email: food@grubstreet.co.uk

Design by Roberta Batchelor
Photography by Mark Burstyn
Food and prop styling by Jennifer Low
All props privately owned by Kitchen for Kids www.kitchenforkids.com
Recipe on cover: Tea Party Vanilla Cupcake, Tea Party Icing

Copyright this edition © Grub Street 2005
Text copyright © Jennifer Low 2004
First published in Canada as Kitchen for Kids by Whitecap

British Library Cataloguing in Publication Data

Low, Jennifer
 Kids' kitchen
1. Cookery
I.Title
641.5'123
ISBN-10: 1 904943 14 4
ISBN-13: 978 1 904943 14 3

For my sweethearts,
whose love makes everything
worthwhile

My extraordinary husband, John,
my wondrous children, Lee and Livvy,
and our faithful companion,
Bailey

Printed and bound in India

Acknowledgements

Kids Kitchen was the book I wanted to find for my children — a *real* cookbook brimming with recipes designed just for them. It would reflect a chef's world as dreamed up by a child. I searched for it, but it didn't exist. Still, I hoped that someone would write it, then I could just buy a copy to use. But that didn't happen. As fate would have it, I bumped into Robert McCullough, Whitecap's director of publishing, at a party and we got to talking. He quickly understood the place *Kids Kitchen* would find in readers' lives. Since that meeting, we have shared many ideas (and a few laughs) and I want to thank him for being *Kids Kitchen's* astute shepherd through the publishing world.

I think I now know why this book wasn't done before. I have two young children. As any parent knows, it's impossible to work with any meaningful degree of focus when little ones are underfoot. And, yet, it's during these early years, when they are most curious and want a hand in absolutely everything, that this book would be most useful. So there's the predicament. I could envision the book, but to create it certainly meant countless hours designing recipes. As a busy working mum, how would I ever find time for it? Which brings me to my wonderful husband, John Southerst. While I tested recipes and wrote, month after month, he shouldered all the responsibilities of SuperDad: piano and football lessons, day trips, grocery shopping, play dates, meals, dishes, laundry and on and on. John didn't even complain (well, not too loudly anyway) when our kitchen began to resemble a bakery. Without my husband's mighty effort and unqualified support, this book simply would not have been possible. My most heartfelt thank you goes to him.

During the recipe testing process, I also enlisted the aid of dozens of parents who carefully recorded their childrens' comments as they put recipes through their paces. I want to thank them all for their time, observations and ideas, but I would especially like to thank Anne Pengelly, my "Aussie Connection," who spread the word for me Down Under and diligently researched my every query. Thanks also go to my talented and unflappable editor, Alison Maclean, who not only tweaked the copy until it was just right, she volunteered her own kids to test recipes. The Bent-Ear Award goes to my sister, Shirley Low, for letting me bounce batches of ideas off her. And a hug and thank you to my friend Veronika Martenova Charles, who has shared her experience of being a children's book author with me over the years and let me benefit from her wisdom.

Of course, making a cookbook for children is only half done when the words are finished. A big thank you goes to photographer

Mark Burstyn for his talent and tireless dedication to every shot. He has truly created a little world apart. And thanks to Kerry Burstyn for her support and advice. Thank you to Roberta Batchelor for designing such a beautiful book and patiently leafing through my paint chips. And hats off to all the staff at Whitecap who worked so hard to make this huge project happen. Grateful thanks also go to Lynda Reeves and Cobi Ladner, who generously granted me a leave from my position as food editor at *House & Home* magazine to put the final push on the manuscript.

And finally, my biggest thank you goes to the *Kids* Kitchen testers (ages 4 to 11), who bowled me over with their hard work, enthusiasm and pride in making every recipe even better. Their excitement was my great reward. To me, their names form a rollof honour They are:

Nicholas and Nathan Anderson; Emma and Zachary Armstrong; Daina Cers; Aidan Chamandy; Frankie Cook; Alexander and Kathryn Crosby; Hannah and Merin Denson; Max, Tiger and Duncan Durie; Rebecca Evans; Allison and Rachel Finer; Rachel Forbes; Nicki and Sophia Forster; Alison and Megan French; Nicholas Hadas; Jacob Harding; Adam and Nicholas Hardy; Rachel and Sarah Harrison; Samantha Hassal; Emily Hickey; Quinlan Hickey; Hannah and Charlie Johnston; Cameron and Jarrett King; Stephanie and Kiarra Lau; Sydney Lau; Jason Mah; Misha Makarewicz; Samantha, Katie and Erin Mason; Rachel and Evan Mazierski; Lisa Mochrie; Sophia and Natalya Motluk; Victoria Myers; Kimberly and Maxwell Ng; Kaylin Rabe; Madeline and Emily Rosen; Kate Sandercock; Christopher Sargent; Cailey Scherer; Lena Sarchuk and Kai MacRae Sigurdson; Mackenzie Smedmor; Christian and Victoria V. Smith; Daniel and Carter Smith; Melissa and Amanda Sorokolit; Nicole and Kate Taylor; Will, Gwyneth and Gareth Thorlakson; Alison Traub; Rachel and Victoria Troke; Elizabeth Wigle; David Wood and Avril Wu.

Great job, kids!
Jennifer

Introduction

No young person should pass through childhood without making a loaf of bread or a cake. So sad to miss out on stirring a fragrant bowl of dough or knowing the heavenly taste of oven-fresh baking. The yeasty aroma of bread, the singular richness of a homemade cake. These things imprint on the memory. Food becomes wonderment. Cooking is magical.

This book contains more than 100 easy recipes specially designed for children to make. Written by a mother with young children, it's the only cookbook where children do not need to use sharp knives or small electric appliances. They also do not cook at oven-top rings or burners. Yet they will be able to make amazing treats, snacks and meals.

Every recipe has been successfully tested by 4 to 11 year olds. Some your child may need to grow into, others enable even the youngest to make something lovely to eat. Each is an authentic recipe made simple enough for the smallest of hands. Years of testing has produced pastry that won't toughen on handling like traditional doughs, a fool-proof trick to make bread dough stretchy without long risings, pasta and noodle recipes that cook perfectly without a pot of boiling water. Your child will discover how to make trays of delicate cream puffs, savoury dumplings, cozy little shepherd's pies and cookies shaped like lollipops. And they'll be delighted that they can make all these delicious things so easily.

Mostly, this is a book about *doing*. Measuring, mixing, rolling, sprinkling — and much peering excitedly through the oven window. It's hard to say which part your child will love the most. Adult supervision and some assistance are suggested, but the recipes are designed to let children do most of the work — and let their sense of accomplishment grow.

The recipes yield small batches. (Of course, you can make multiples if you wish for more to share.) Smaller quantities are easier for children to handle. In fact, no recipe in the book requires more than two eggs. That means they can bake to their hearts' content and you'll still have enough eggs left for breakfast. And as for the children…they will be left with memories to last a lifetime.

Happy cooking,
Jennifer Low

Organizing the Kitchen

Getting Ready

The idea behind *Kids Kitchen* is that this is truly a cookbook for children. Let your kids be in charge of their cooking project, selecting which recipe to make, gathering supplies and measuring ingredients, then actually preparing the recipe themselves. Every recipe has a photo to help explain what the end result should be.

While all the recipes are designed for children to make, supervision by an adult is suggested. Since you know your child's skills best, you determine how much help your child will need. No recipes require the use of sharp knives or cooking over heat, so you will be pleasantly surprised at how much children will be able to do by themselves.

A couple of practical points to note:

First, read the recipe before you start. Make sure you have the necessary ingredients and supplies so your time together isn't interrupted by an emergency trip to the supermarket. It's a good idea to set the ingredients out before starting so there are no surprises.

Second, read the rest of the instructions in this chapter, especially "Measuring Ingredients," before rolling up your sleeves. Once you know the *Kids Kitchen* methods, you will get the best results.

A few recipes offer 2 batch sizes so you can choose the amount you want to make.

Now you're ready to begin. The recipes are meant to be read aloud by an adult to a child. Let your child finish each task before you read the next step. Older children may be able to read the directions themselves, but you should be in the kitchen to offer help or explanation.

Preparing Tins

Round cake tins and round metal pans: These should be greased, floured and lined to ensure cakes unmold easily.

Grease and flour the tin before lining it. To grease, brush the sides with a pastry brush dipped in butter, margarine or vegetable oil, or rub on with a bunched piece of plastic wrap, or simply use the paper wrapper left over from butter. For tart rings and pans, only the sides need to be greased.

To flour, spoon a little flour into the greased tin. Tip or roll the tin around until a fine coating of flour covers all the grease. Tap out the extra flour into the sink.

To line a round tin, trace the bottom of the tin onto a piece of greaseproof or parchment paper. Cut out the circle of paper slightly smaller than the tracing to fit flat in the bottom of the tin.

Square and rectangular tins: It is often sufficient to grease and line these (no flouring).

For square and rectangular tins, it's best to grease both the sides and bottoms. The grease helps hold the parchment paper in place for spreading stiff batters or doughs. To grease, brush with a light coating of butter, margarine or vegetable oil with a pastry brush or rub on with a bunched piece of plastic wrap, or simply use the paper wrapper left over from butter.

To line a square or rectangular tin, cut a piece of parchment paper wide enough to cover the bottom and long enough to hang over two sides. The overhang makes it easier to lift cakes or squares out of the tin. Fold the paper to fit snugly into the corners.

Baking sheets: To line, cut a piece of greaseproof paper to fit inside the baking sheet. This will prevent doughs from sticking.

Measuring Ingredients

It is essential to measure flour properly. The simplest way to measure dry ingredients is with a measuring jug or a set of measuring cups. Measuring cups make measuring flour very easy for smaller children and a plastic set can be purchased for a few pounds (Lakeland Limited shops are especially good for all cookware needs and they have a website where you can buy). The correct method is to **stir your bag or canister of flour, transfer heaped spoonfuls into your measuring jug and shake til the level is even or with a measuring cup level off with a dinner or palette knife,** if that is the method you are using. With measuring spoons, it is fine to scoop them into the flour and level off with a dinner knife or palette knife.

When measuring icing sugar or unsweetened cocoa powder, follow the same method as for flour. Icing sugar and cocoa powder can be lumpy, so you will need to lightly "chop" the lumps to break them up as you level them off.

To avoid ruining your recipe, do not measure ingredients over your mixing bowl. Spills cannot be removed from batters. Instead, measure over an empty bowl to catch drips.

To help kids measure out small quantities of liquids, transfer the liquids to smaller containers. For instance, vegetable oil can be funnelled into small bottles fitted with pouring spouts. Milk can be poured from large cartons into cups. Also, with new bottles of flavourings or vinegar, do not remove the foil cover on the opening. Instead, pierce a small hole through the foil to create a manageable flow.

Working with Yeast and Butter

All the yeasted recipes use the quick-rise variety (see Glossary). For bread-making, the yeast needs to be foamed before adding to recipes. To do this, sprinkle the yeast over the "very warm" water specified in the recipe, with any sugar specified. Use a small cup to hold this mixture since a larger cup or bowl will let the water cool too quickly. "Very warm" water should be as warm as possible while still comfortable to the touch. If the water is too cold, the yeast will not foam. But if it is too hot, it will kill the yeast. The sugar helps the yeast to grow. After adding the yeast and sugar to the water, jiggle the cup slightly to moisten them. Let stand at least 10 minutes for the mix to turn foamy (see photo above). Add all of the foam and water to the recipes. Not a lot of yeast is used, so be sure to scrape the cup to get all of it into the recipe.

If your kitchen does not have a warm enough spot for dough to rise, make a warm spot by placing the plastic-covered bowl on top of (not inside) an oven set at 300°F to 350°F (150°C to 180°C). Check that there are no hot spots on the bowl (from hot air blowing out of the oven vents). The bowl should feel comfortably warm to the touch. A metal mixing bowl works best for rising dough since it warms quickly.

Soft butter is often called for in cake and cookie recipes. Let cold butter stand at room temperature for several hours or overnight to soften. It should be soft enough to easily mix with sugar using a wooden spoon. All recipes call for unsalted butter. Do not substitute salted butter because it will make your food turn out too salty.

Some recipes call for cold butter to be cut into pieces for microwaving. Cut into large chunks to speed melting.

Using Microwave and Regular Ovens

The exposed heat of the cooker is never used by kids in these recipes. Ingredients are heated in the microwave oven instead.

All bowls and cups used in the microwave must be microwave safe.

The microwave is usually used at 50% power in this book. For example, if your microwave levels are 1 to 10, you would use level 5. Heating times may vary due to assorted oven wattages.

Microwave-safe glass bowls are handy since they allow you to watch the ingredients as they heat and you can see when they are melted or bubbling. Glass cups with handles are also good for microwave use since their handles do not get as hot as the sides of bowls.

When baking in a regular oven (not the microwave), use the middle rack.

Supervision and assistance is suggested for removing hot pans or bowls from all ovens.

Basic Tools

Baking spatulas: You might call these rubber spatulas. But baking spatulas are made not only of rubber, but also assorted heatproof materials that allow them to stir hot ingredients without melting. This book occasionally calls for **heatproof baking spatulas** (see photo above), which are usually embossed with a maximum temperature on the blade. When heatproof is not specified, any baking spatula can be used. Large ones are best for mixing and cleaning batter out of bowls. Small spatulas (see photo) are helpful for scraping ingredients out of small bowls.

Bowls for beating egg whites: Only one or two egg whites are required in any recipe, so it's important to put them into a smaller bowl or measuring jug just large enough to fit the beaters. If the bowl is too big, you won't have enough egg white to "catch" in the beaters. The ideal size is a 500-mL liquid measuring jug (see photo above). The egg whites should be beaten until white and fluffy with no liquid egg left in the bottom of the jug.

Egg separator: When egg whites and yolks are used separately, an egg separator can be used to divide them. Some types clip to bowl rims (see photo above), while others are balanced across the top of a bowl. Crack an egg and split the shell over the egg separator. The yolk will sit in the separator while the egg white drains out the bottom slats into the bowl or cup below.

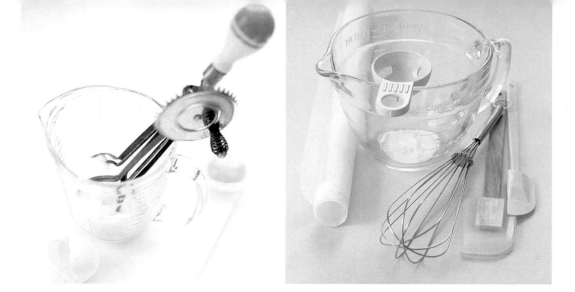

If you do not have a separator, older children may be able to divide eggs by splitting the shell in half and passing the egg yolk back and forth between the half shells, allowing the egg white to drip into a bowl below. Do not let any yolk remain in the egg whites or they cannot be beaten fluffy. If yolk does get into the egg white, carefully scoop the spots out using the eggshell. However, it is not a problem if egg whites get stuck on yolks.

Mixing bowls: High-sided bowls prevent ingredients from sliding out while mixing. Some also have spouts, handy for pouring batter. Some mixing bowls have non-skid rubber bottoms, but you can lay a damp tea towel under bowls to prevent slipping.

Parchment or greaseproof paper: Baked goods won't stick to baking trays if you line them with parchment paper, also called baking paper or silicone paper. It is commonly available in rolls in white or brown. It can be wiped down with a damp tea towel and re-used several times if it isn't too messy.

Rotary egg-beater: Since no small electric appliances are used in this book, a manually operated rotary egg-beater is used for beating fluffy eggs. Younger children may need help with this, or adults can assist by whipping the eggs with an electric beater.

Whisk: The whisk required for these recipes is the common balloon whisk (see photo above). Unlike in adult recipes, it is not used for whipping ingredients. Instead, the recipes most often use the whisk for stirring. A stiff whisk works best. Be sure it is not too long for your child to handle comfortably.

Breakfast, Lunch and Dinner

1

Oatmeal Nut Granola

This is a crunchy breakfast cereal that tastes like a classic cookie.

Supplies

baking sheet with shallow sides, parchment paper, spoon, bowls, measuring jug and spoons

Ingredients

300 mL (1¼ cups) rolled oats (quick-cooking, but not instant)

4 Tbsp unsalted sunflower seeds

4 Tbsp sliced almonds, if you wish

4 Tbsp dried cranberries or raisins

2 Tbsp wheat germ

4 Tbsp unsalted butter, cut into pieces

4 Tbsp honey

1 Tbsp light muscovado brown sugar

¼ tsp cinnamon

3 or 4 drops of vanilla extract

pinch of salt

cold milk, to serve

1 Preheat oven to 300°F (150°C).

2 Line a baking sheet with parchment paper.

3 Spread the rolled oats, sunflower seeds and almonds, if using, on the sheet and bake 5 minutes. Remove from the oven (but leave the oven on). Cool the mix. Lift up the parchment and pour the oats and nuts into a bowl. Stir in the dried cranberries or raisins and wheat germ.

4 In a small bowl, melt the butter at 50% power in the microwave (about 1 minute). Mix in the honey, brown sugar, cinnamon, vanilla and salt. Pour over the rolled oats and mix to coat.

5 Return the parchment paper to the baking sheet. Pour the granola mix onto the sheet and spread out evenly. Return to the oven and bake 20 minutes. Take the granola out of the oven, stir it around, then return it to the oven to bake for another 5 to 10 minutes. Watch carefully that the granola turns golden, but not too brown. Cool completely on the baking sheet. The granola will be soft when just out of the oven, but will harden as it cools. After it hardens, break it up into small pieces with your hands. Eat with cold milk.

Makes 625 mL Oatmeal Nut Granola.

Oatmeal Nut Granola

Noisy French Toast

Blueberry Muffins with Cinnamon Sugar

Noisy French Toast

This French toast crunches when you bite into it, but it's crisp only on the outside. Inside, the bread is soft and eggy.

Supplies

baking sheet, parchment paper, measuring jug and spoons, heavy plastic bag, rolling pin or coffee mug, 2 pie dishes or shallow dishes, bowl, whisk, fork, tongs or cooking spatula

Ingredients

2 or 3 slices of wholewheat bread

250 mL (1 cup) cornflakes

2 large eggs

5 Tbsp milk

1/2 tsp plain flour

2 drops of vanilla extract

butter and golden syrup, for serving

1 Line a baking sheet with parchment paper.

2 Get help cutting the bread slices into quarters.

3 Preheat oven to 400°F (200°C).

4 Put the bread pieces on the lined sheet into the warming oven (it does not need to be at full temperature) for 5 minutes to toast lightly. Cool the bread completely.

5 Seal the cornflakes in a heavy plastic bag. Crush them with a rolling pin or coffee mug to the size of rolled oats. Pour into a pie dish or shallow dish.

6 In a large bowl, use a whisk to mix the eggs, milk, flour and vanilla until blended. Be sure there are no lumps of unmixed flour. Pour into a shallow dish.

7 In batches, lay the bread pieces in the egg mix. Soak about 2 minutes, then turn over and soak another 2 minutes in the egg. Be careful not to rip the bread. It will be soft and soggy. You might need to lift the pieces with a fork.

8 Place the bread pieces in the cornflake crumbs. Coat both sides. Place on the lined baking sheet. Bake 10 minutes, then flip over with tongs and bake another 5 to 10 minutes, until the crumbs begin to turn brown. Eat warm with butter and pancake syrup.

Makes 2 or 3 servings of Noisy French Toast.

Blueberry Muffins
with Cinnamon Sugar

Loaded with blueberries, these lovely muffins are almost cake-like.

Supplies
12 hole muffin tin, bowls, measuring jug and spoons, whisk, baking spatula, 2 teaspoons

Ingredients
375 mL (1$\frac{1}{2}$ cups) plain flour

175 mL ($\frac{3}{4}$ cup) golden granulated sugar

2 tsp baking powder

$\frac{1}{4}$ tsp bicarbonate of soda

$\frac{1}{8}$ tsp salt

1$\frac{1}{2}$ tsp golden granulated sugar

$\frac{1}{2}$ tsp cinnamon

1 large egg

4 Tbsp milk

4 Tbsp vegetable oil

1 Tbsp lemon juice

175 mL ($\frac{3}{4}$ cup) fresh or frozen blueberries

1 Preheat oven to 375°F (190°C).

2 Grease the muffin tin.

3 Mix the flour, sugar, baking powder, bicarbonate of soda and salt in a bowl. Set aside.

4 In a small bowl or cup, mix the 1$\frac{1}{2}$ tsp sugar and cinnamon. Set aside.

5 In another bowl, use a whisk to stir the egg, milk, oil and lemon juice until smooth. Switch to a baking spatula and scrape into the flour mixture. Stir to form a stiff batter. Don't overmix. Stir in the blueberries. (Be especially careful not to overmix frozen blueberries because the juice will make the batter green.)

6 Grease a teaspoon to scoop the stiff batter into 9 holes of the muffin tin to about half-full. Use a clean teaspoon to sprinkle the cinnamon sugar on top.

7 Bake about 20 minutes, or until the muffins are puffed and golden. Cool slightly. Eat while warm.

Makes 9 Blueberry Muffins with Cinnamon Sugar.

Tuna Fish Patties

Crunchy on the outside, tender and full of flavour on the inside, these patties are like a tuna version of restaurant fish cakes.

Supplies

baking sheet, parchment paper, measuring jug and spoons, heavy plastic bag, rolling pin or coffee mug, bowls, fork or pastry blender

Ingredients

375 mL (1 1/2 cups) cornflakes

1 tsp vegetable oil

170g tin of tuna

about 10 savoury salted biscuits such as TUC biscuits for 125 mL (1/2 cup) of crumbs

2 large egg whites

3 Tbsp mayonnaise

1 tsp Worcestershire sauce

1 tsp onion salt

1/4 tsp dried dill

1/4 tsp dried oregano

pinch of pepper

1 Preheat oven to 350°F (180°C).

2 Line a baking sheet with parchment paper.

3 Seal the cornflakes in a heavy plastic bag. Crush them with a rolling pin or coffee mug to the size of rolled oats. Pour into a bowl. Drizzle in the vegetable oil and stir with a fork to coat. Set aside.

4 Get help opening and draining the can of tuna. Put the tuna into a bowl and mash into small flakes with a fork or pastry blender.

5 Put the biscuits in the plastic bag and crush the same way as the cornflakes. Add the biscuit crumbs to the bowl of tuna. Except for the cornflakes, add the rest of the ingredients and mix well with a fork.

6 Shape the tuna into four 2.5-cm thick patties. Roll the patties in the cornflake crumbs to coat all sides. Place on the lined baking sheet. Bake about 25 minutes, until the cornflake crumbs are lightly browned.

Makes 4 Tuna Fish Patties.

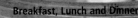

Two Cheese Penne Pasta

Tuna Fish Patties

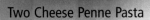

Paddy Thai Noodles

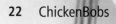

Paddy Thai Noodles

Plan ahead to allow at least 1 hour for the noodles to soak. Then you're set to make this children's version of Pad Thai, a popular restaurant dish.

Supplies

large metal mixing bowl (about 2.5-L capacity), heavy bowl, colander, measuring jug and spoons, tongs or wooden spoon, foil, pizza cutter, kitchen scissors

Ingredients

175 to 200 g uncooked flat rice noodles
(5-mm wide)

125 mL ketchup

125 mL water

2 Tbsp vegetable oil

1 Tbsp soy sauce

1 tsp garlic salt

1/2 tsp ground coriander

a few drops of sesame oil, if you wish

Any or all of the following toppings

2 or 3 slices of cold chicken

115 g cooked, peeled prawns, frozen or thawed

1/2 spring onion

handful of raw bean sprouts

chopped peanuts for sprinkling

1 Put the noodles in a large metal mixing bowl. Break them up if they stick out of the bowl. Put the bowl in the sink and add enough very warm (but not hot) water to cover the noodles. Place a heavy bowl on top to keep the noodles in the water and soak at least 1 hour (up to 3 hours) to soften. Drain in a colander.

2 Preheat the oven to 350°F (180°C).

3 In the metal mixing bowl (now empty), mix the ketchup, water, oil, soy sauce, salt, coriander and sesame oil, if using.

4 Add the noodles to the bowl. Mix with tongs or a wooden spoon to coat with the ketchup sauce. Cover tightly with foil and bake 30 minutes. Get help taking the bowl out and opening the foil. (Leave oven on.)

5 Use the tongs or wooden spoon to mix the noodles again. Lift the softer noodles to the top so the stiffer ones can reach the sauce in the bottom. Re-cover with the foil and bake another 10 minutes. Remove from oven (keep oven on) and carefully taste to check for tenderness. Noodles should be soft. If they are too hard and chewy, mix in 2 Tbsp water, cover and bake another 10 minutes or until soft.

6 If you are adding the chicken, use a pizza cutter to slice it into thin strips. Add the chicken and prawns. Cover the bowl with foil. Bake another 10 minutes.

7 Spoon Paddy Thai into serving dishes and sprinkle with spring onion (snipped into pieces with scissors), bean sprouts and chopped peanuts, if you wish.

Makes 3 or 4 small servings of Paddy Thai Noodles.

Two Cheese Penne Pasta

No oven-top boiling needed! Uncooked pasta turns tender as it bakes in chicken stock and cheese. Penne are straight pasta tubes about the diameter of a pencil.

Supplies

bowls, measuring jug and spoons, whisk, colander, spoon, 1.5-L baking dish with lid

Ingredients

500 mL (140 g or 2 cups) uncooked penne pasta

1 Tbsp olive oil

500 mL very warm water

250 mL chicken or vegetable stock

125 mL whipping cream

5 Tbsp grated Parmesan cheese

5 Tbsp ricotta cheese

1/2 tsp dried basil

1/2 tsp garlic salt

pinch of pepper

pinch of nutmeg, if you wish

5 Tbsp ricotta cheese

1 In a bowl, mix the penne, olive oil and very warm water. Let stand for 30 minutes to soften the pasta.

2 Preheat oven to 425°F (220°C).

3 In another bowl, use a whisk to mix the stock, cream, Parmesan, ricotta, basil, salt, pepper and, if you wish, nutmeg.

4 Drain the pasta in a colander. Stir the pasta into the cream mixture. Pour the pasta and creamy liquid into the baking dish. Spread the pasta evenly.

5 Use a spoon to drop the ricotta in 5 small blobs onto the pasta. (Don't stir.) Cover the dish with its lid. Bake 45 minutes, until the sauce is bubbling and the pasta is tender.

Makes 4 servings of Two Cheese Penne Pasta.

ChickenBobs

When was the last time you ate lunch or dinner on a stick? These chicken balls are baked on wooden sticks, ready for dipping into ketchup or plum sauce.

Supplies

baking sheet, parchment paper, heavy plastic bag, measuring jug and spoons, rolling pin or coffee mug, bowls, 10 wooden sticks

Ingredients

175 mL (3 or 4 handfuls) potato crisps

250 g uncooked minced chicken

4 Tbsp bread crumbs

1 Tbsp dried onion flakes

1 Tbsp ketchup

1/2 tsp dried oregano

1/4 tsp chilli powder

1/4 tsp garlic salt

ketchup or plum sauce for dipping, if you wish

1 Preheat oven to 375°F (190°C).

2 Line a baking sheet with parchment paper.

3 Put 3 or 4 handfuls of crisps into a heavy plastic bag and tie it up. Use a rolling pin or the bottom of a coffee mug to crush the crisps into little pieces about the size of rolled oats. Pour into a small bowl.

4 Mix the chicken, bread crumbs, onion flakes, ketchup, oregano, chilli powder (but not the crisps) into a bowl. Use your hands to mix the ingredients. Wash your hands.

5 Fill a large bowl with cold water. Dip your hands in the water first, then roll the chicken into balls the size of big walnuts. (The water stops the chicken from sticking to your hands.) Next, roll each ball in the crushed potato crisps, covering completely. Make 10 balls.

6 Place the balls on the lined baking sheet. Wash your hands. Press a wooden stick through each ball all the way to the bottom.

7 Bake about 30 minutes, until the crisp coating is lightly browned. Get help cutting a ChickenBob to check that they're cooked through. Cool until warm before eating. Dip into ketchup or plum sauce to eat, if you wish.

Makes 10 ChickenBobs.

Dumpling Raviolis

Dumpling Raviolis

These are like wontons. Most of the fun is in making them, but you'll need help cooking them.

Supplies

kitchen scissors, bowls, measuring jug and spoons, fork, pastry brush, large pot and slotted spoon or skimmer to be used by helper

Ingredients

1/2 spring onion

175 g uncooked minced pork or chicken

1/2 tsp soy sauce

1/2 tsp vegetable oil

1 tsp garlic salt

pinch of pepper

1 large egg white

32 wonton wrappers (one pack)

1.5 L water for cooking

soy sauce for serving

1 Use kitchen scissors to snip the spring onion into small pieces. You'll have about 3 Tbsp.

2 Put the spring onion, minced meat, soy sauce, oil, salt and pepper in a bowl and mix well with a fork.

3 Put the egg white into a small bowl and beat lightly with a fork.

4 Lay a wonton wrapper flat on your work surface. Place a slightly rounded teaspoon of the meat in the middle of it. (Don't add too much or it will be hard to wrap.) Dip a pastry brush into the egg white and brush it on the wrapper around the meat and right over the edges of the wrapper.

5 Place another wrapper over the one with the meat, lining up the corners. Press the 2 wrappers together, but don't press on the meat. As you're pressing the wrappers together, push out big air bubbles inside. Make 16 raviolis.

6 Let a grown-up cook the raviolis in a pot of simmering water on the stove. Put 5 or 6 in the pot at a time and simmer for about 10 minutes, turning occasionally. Use a slotted spoon or skimmer to lift them into serving bowls. Add a few drops of soy sauce. Eat while warm.

Makes 16 Dumpling Raviolis.

Perfect Crust Pizzas

Make a crust from scratch and you'll never forget how good it is! Plus, a pizzeria secret: use both Cheddar and Mozzarella cheese for the best taste.

Supplies

cup, bowls, measuring jug and spoons, baking spatula or wooden spoon, plastic wrap, 2 baking sheets or pizza pans, spoon

Crust

175 mL very warm, but not hot, water

1 tsp quick-rise yeast

1/2 tsp golden granulated sugar

375 mL (1 1/2 cups) plain flour

1/2 tsp salt

1 tsp olive or vegetable oil

oil for pans

1 tsp cornmeal for sprinkling

Toppings

150 mL tomato sauce

5 Tbsp grated Cheddar cheese

5 Tbsp grated Mozzarella cheese

(or use Mozzarella only, if you wish)

your choice of other toppings: pepperoni, ham slices, pineapple pieces, bell peppers, tomatoes, onions, olives (Get help cutting up these toppings.)

1 For the crust, put the water, yeast and sugar in a cup and jiggle to blend. Do not stir. Let stand at least 10 minutes to get foamy.

2 In a large bowl, mix the flour and salt. Add the yeast and the teaspoon of oil. Stir with a baking spatula or wooden spoon until you have a smooth, sticky dough. Cover the bowl with plastic wrap and set in a warm place to rise 30 minutes.

3 Preheat oven to 400°F (200°C).

4 You will make two 20-cm diameter pizzas. Rub your baking sheets or pizza pans with a drizzle of oil. Use a spoon to sprinkle cornmeal over the oil. This helps to keep the crusts from sticking.

5 Use the baking spatula or wooden spoon to scoop out half the risen dough onto each sheet or pan.

6 Rub some oil onto your palms. Press the dough with your fingers into round shapes about 5 mm thick. It is stretchy dough and will spring back as you flatten it, but keep working and the dough will thin out. Don't worry if the pizzas have an odd shape, as long as the dough is about 5 mm thick.

7 Pre-bake the crusts 15 to 17 minutes, until they begin to turn golden. Take out of the oven, but keep the oven on. Cool until just warm so you don't burn yourself when adding toppings.

8 Use the back of a spoon to spread the tomato sauce on the crusts, leaving about 1 cm at the edges. Sprinkle on the cheeses and any toppings you like. Return to the oven for about 10 minutes, or until the cheeses are melted, slightly bubbling, and the edges of the crusts are golden. Eat while warm.

Makes 2 Perfect Crust Pizzas.

Chicken in Crunchy Coats

These oven-cooked drumsticks are made with the skinless drumsticks sold in many supermarkets. The delicious crunchy coating covers moist, tender chicken.

Supplies

baking sheet, parchment paper, bowls, measuring jug and spoons, cup, fork, 2 plates or shallow dishes, baking pan

Ingredients

6 to 8 skinless chicken drumsticks (100 g each)

125 mL (1/2 cup) bread crumbs

4 Tbsp grated Parmesan cheese

2 Tbsp plain flour

1 tsp garlic salt

1 tsp dried parsley

1 tsp dried thyme

1/2 tsp paprika

1/4 tsp white or black pepper

3 Tbsp (45 g) unsalted butter

5 Tbsp milk

5 Tbsp plain flour

1 Preheat oven to 400°F (200°C).

2 Line a baking sheet with parchment paper.

3 In a bowl, mix the bread crumbs, Parmesan, flour, salt, parsley, salt, thyme, paprika and pepper.

4 Put the butter in a cup and melt at 50% power in the microwave (about 30 seconds). Drizzle the melted butter over the bread crumb mixture and stir with a fork to coat the crumbs. Use the back of the fork to mash any lumps. Pour onto a plate or shallow dish.

5 Into another plate or dish, sprinkle the 5 Tbsp flour.

6 Put the drumsticks in a baking pan just large enough to hold them in a single layer. Pour the milk over them. Roll the drumsticks in the milk to coat them. Holding each drumstick by the bone end, roll it in the flour until it is completely coated. Then roll the flour-coated chicken back in the milk. Be sure the milk soaks all the flour. Now roll the chicken in the bread crumb mixture to completely coat. You'll need to wash your hands between rolling drumsticks since your fingers will get a thick coating, too.

7 Place drumsticks on the lined baking sheet. Bake 45 to 50 minutes. The drumsticks are done when they are not pink inside. Get help to check inside the chicken.

Makes 6 to 8 pieces of Chicken in Crunchy Coats.

Sugared Baby Carrots

An easy way to cook a side dish from the peeled baby carrots sold by the bag in supermarkets. Cook in the same oven as the Chicken in Crunchy Coats (page 30), but for a slightly shorter time.

Supplies
bowl, measuring spoons, foil

Ingredients
about 15 baby carrots
1 tsp vegetable oil
$1/2$ tsp light muscovado brown sugar
pinch of chilli powder
1 ice cube

1 Preheat oven to 400°F (200°C).

2 Mix the carrots, oil, brown sugar and chilli powder in a bowl.

3 Rip 2 large squares of foil about 30 cm square. Place the coated carrots and an ice cube on 1 piece of foil. Cover with the other piece. Roll up the 4 edges to make a sealed packet.

4 Bake 40 minutes. Get help opening the foil and spooning the carrots onto plates. Eat while warm.

Makes 1 packet Sugared Baby Carrots.

Chicken in Crunchy Coats, Sugared Baby Carrots   Peek-a-Boo Meatloaf, Peas and Corn Packets

Peek-a-Boo Meatloaf

This makes just enough for 2 or 3 kids' dinners or to tuck into sandwiches for lunch. Peas and Corn Packets (page 34) can be made in the same oven, but for a shorter time.

Supplies

large bowl, measuring spoons, 15 x 8-cm mini-loaf tin, fork, spoon

Ingredients

250 g uncooked minced beef

1 large egg white

2 Tbsp bread crumbs

1 Tbsp ketchup

1 tsp dried onion flakes

$1/2$ tsp garlic salt

$1/4$ tsp chilli powder

$1/4$ tsp dry mustard

$1/4$ tsp Worcestershire sauce

sprinkle of pepper

1 hot dog sausage

1 Tbsp chilli sauce

1 Preheat oven to 350°F (180°C).

2 Put all the ingredients — except the hot dog and chilli sauce — into a large bowl. Use your hands to mix the ingredients together well.

3 Firmly press about $1/3$ of the mixture into the bottom of the mini-loaf tin. Pierce the hot dog 6 times with a fork. Place it in the middle of the loaf. Firmly press the rest of the meat on top, covering the hot dog completely. Use the back of a spoon to spread the chilli sauce on top.

4 Bake 40 minutes, or until the top of the meatloaf is browned and juices around the edge are bubbling. Cool slightly before eating.

Makes 1 Peek-a-Boo Meatloaf.

Peas and Corn Packets

Ice cubes are used to steam sugar snap peas and baby corn in the oven, a neat trick! Make these in the same oven as the Peek-a-Boo Meatloaf (page 33), but for less time.

Supplies

bowl, measuring spoons, spoon, foil, baking sheet

Ingredients

16 fresh sugar snap peas

10 fresh whole baby corn cobs

4 Tbsp frozen peas

1 tsp vegetable oil

$\frac{1}{2}$ tsp soy sauce

pinch of garlic salt

sprinkle of pepper

2 ice cubes

1   Preheat oven to 350°F (180°C).

2   Wash the sugar snaps. Trim them by snapping off the stems and pulling off the long stringy skin that runs along the edge. Put the trimmed sugar snaps into a bowl. (Throw out the stems and stringy bits.)

3   Rinse the baby corns. Add with the frozen peas to the bowl of sugar snaps. Add the oil, soy sauce, salt and pepper. Use a spoon to stir well.

4   Cut 2 squares of foil, each about 30 cm square. Lay the squares on your work table. Put a pile of the vegetables in the middle of each square. Add an ice cube to each pile.

5   Wrap the foil around the veggies and ice, sealing the edges. Make sure there are no holes. Place on a baking sheet. Bake 20 minutes.

6   Get help opening a packet to check that the sugar snaps are cooked. They should be bright green, crunchy but not raw. When the sugar snaps are done, the baby corn and shelled peas will also be ready. Eat warm.

Makes 2 Peas and Corn Packets.

Wee Shepherd's Pies

These pies may be small, but they are surprisingly filling. The little tins are available in kitchenware shops and with the disposable aluminium bakeware sold in supermarkets.

Supplies

shallow bowl or dish, bowls, wooden spoon or potato masher, spoons, measuring jug and spoons, two or three 12-cm diameter pie dishes, baking sheet

Ingredients

250 g uncooked lean minced beef

2 tsp cornflour

1 Tbsp ketchup

2 tsp dried onion flakes

1/4 tsp salt

pinch of pepper

4 Tbsp frozen sweetcorn kernels or peas

175 mL milk

175 mL water

1 Tbsp unsalted butter

1/4 tsp salt

250 mL (1 cup) instant potato powder

1 large egg yolk

1 Preheat oven to 375°F (190°C).

2 Break up the minced beef into a shallow bowl or dish. Heat at 50% power in a microwave for about 3 minutes. Don't worry if the beef is not completely cooked yet. Spoon the beef into another bowl, leaving behind the fat. Throw away the fat.

3 Use the back of a wooden spoon or a potato masher to break up the beef into small pieces. Use a spoon to sprinkle the cornflour over the beef and stir until no powder can be seen anymore. Mix in the ketchup, onion flakes, salt, pepper and frozen sweetcorn or peas.

4 Spread evenly in 2 or 3 of the small pie dishes.

5 Put the milk, water, butter and salt in a bowl. Heat at 50% power in a microwave for about 3 minutes, or until the mix is hot. Use a clean spoon to stir in the instant potato until smooth. Then stir in the egg yolk. Mix well. Spoon the potato over the beef and use the back of the spoon to spread the potato to the edges of the pans.

6 Place the pies on a baking sheet. Bake about 30 minutes, or until the potato begins to turn golden. Cool slightly before eating.

Makes 2 or 3 Wee Shepherd's Pies.

Wee Shepherd's Pies

Baker's Meatballs

Baker's Meatballs

This recipe makes about 14 meatballs, maybe even a couple more.
Eat them with some vegetables or add them to a spaghetti dinner. Get help warming
tomato sauce to serve with them, if you wish.

Supplies

baking sheet with shallow sides, foil, baking rack,
bowls, measuring jug and spoons

Ingredients

500 g uncooked minced beef (or
half beef and half pork)

1 large egg

3 Tbsp bread crumbs

3 Tbsp grated Parmesan cheese

1 Tbsp ketchup

2 tsp dried onion flakes

1 tsp dried oregano

1/2 tsp garlic salt

1/2 tsp Worcestershire sauce

1/4 tsp dry mustard

pinch of pepper

1. Preheat oven to 375°F (190°C).

2. Line a baking sheet with foil. Place baking rack in it.

3. In a big bowl, use your hands to crumble up the minced meat. Wash your hands. Crack the egg into the bowl. Add the rest of the ingredients. Mix well with your hands. Wash your hands.

4. Press a mound of meat into a tablespoon. It should be rounded over the top of the spoon. Push the meat out of the spoon and roll it into a ball. Make about 14 meatballs. Set them on the baking rack.

5. Put the baking sheet with the rack of meatballs in the oven. Bake 30 to 35 minutes, or until the meatballs are browned and cooked through.

Makes 1 batch Baker's Meatballs.

Breads and Crackers

Banana Fudge Bread

Banana Fudge Bread

You can make this tasty banana bread with or without the fudge swirl,
or with or without nuts.

Supplies

20 x 10-cm loaf tin, bowls, measuring jug and spoons,
sieve, fork or potato masher, baking spatula or wood-
en spoon, dinner knife

Ingredients

375 mL (1^1/$_2$ cups) plain flour

1 tsp bicarbonate of soda

pinch of salt

1 square semi-sweet chocolate, if you wish
   (30 g)

2 ripe bananas

150 mL (^{2}/$_3$ cup) golden granulated sugar

5 Tbsp (75 g) unsalted butter, soft

1 large egg

4 Tbsp milk

1 tsp white vinegar

3 Tbsp chopped walnuts, if you wish

1 Preheat oven to 350°F (180°C).

2 Grease the loaf tin.

3 Into a large bowl, sift and mix the flour, bicarbonate
of soda and salt. Set aside.

4 If making the fudge swirl, put the chocolate in a
bowl and heat at 50% power in the microwave
until melted (about 2 minutes). Set aside.

5 Put the peeled bananas in a bowl and mash with a
fork or potato masher.

6 In another bowl, use a baking spatula or wooden
spoon to cream the sugar and butter. Stir in the
mashed bananas, egg, milk and vinegar. Mix well
and pour into the flour mix. Blend well. Stir in the
nuts, if using.

7 For the plain banana bread, simply pour the banana
batter into the loaf tin. For the fudge swirl, mix
150 mL of batter with the melted chocolate. Pour
the fudge batter into the bowl of banana batter. Stir
once to swirl, then pour into the loaf tin.

8 Bake about 55 minutes, or until the loaf is golden
and a skewer inserted into the middle comes out
clean. Cool completely before unmolding. Loosen
the bread with a dinner knife and tip out.

Makes 1 loaf Banana Fudge Bread.

Roly Poly Bread

You can try cocoa powder with chocolate chips or cinnamon with raisins in the filling.

Supplies

20 x 20-cm square cake tin, plastic wrap,
20 x 10-cm loaf tin, cup, measuring jug and spoons,
bowls, whisk or fork, sieve, baking spatula or wooden
spoon, spoon

Bread

4 Tbsp very warm (but not hot) water

1 tsp quick-rise yeast

1 tsp golden granulated sugar

5 Tbsp milk

4 Tbsp (60 g) unsalted butter, cut into pieces

4 Tbsp skimmed milk powder

4 Tbsp golden granulated sugar

1/2 tsp vanilla extract

pinch of salt

1 large egg

425 mL (1¾ cups) plain flour

4 Tbsp plain flour

flour for dusting

Filling

2 tsp golden granulated sugar

1 tsp unsweetened cocoa powder or cinnamon

2 Tbsp (30 g) unsalted butter, soft

3 Tbsp chocolate chips or raisins

1 Line the square tin with plastic wrap, with lots of overhang. Grease the loaf tin.

2 To make the bread, put the water, yeast and 1 tsp sugar in a cup and jiggle to blend. Do not stir. Let stand at least 10 minutes to get foamy.

3 In a bowl, heat the milk and butter at 50% power in the microwave for about 2 minutes, until the butter melts. Use a whisk or fork to mix in the milk powder, sugar, vanilla, and salt until smooth. Cool to barely warm or room temperature.

4 Sift the flour into a bowl (but *not* the 4 Tbsp flour). Set aside.

5 Use a whisk or fork to beat the yeast and egg into the cooled butter mixture. Mix until smooth. Pour into the bowl of sifted flour. Switch to a baking spatula or wooden spoon and mix vigorously into a smooth, stretchy dough. Cover the bowl with plastic wrap and set in a warm spot to rise for 20 minutes.

6 Make the filling by mixing the 2 tsp golden granulated sugar and the cocoa or cinnamon in a cup.

7 After the dough has risen, sprinkle the leftover 4 Tbsp flour into the bowl. Squeeze it into the dough. Cover the dough again with the plastic wrap and let rise about 15 minutes.

8 Preheat oven to 325°F (160°C).

9 Roll the dough into the lined square tin. Press out evenly to the edges of the tin, popping any large air bubbles.

10 Use the back of a spoon to spread the soft butter over the dough. Sprinkle with the cocoa or cinnamon mixture and the chocolate chips or raisins.

11 Keeping the dough in the tin, use the plastic wrap to help you roll it into a cylinder as tightly as you can, without gaps. Put the roll into the greased loaf tin, with the seam (where the roll ends) on the bottom, removing the plastic.

12 Bake 45 to 50 minutes, or until browned. Cool until just slightly warm before slicing.

Makes 1 loaf Roly Poly Bread.

Chocolate Bread

This bread is just lightly sweet, not like cake. It's delicious fresh from the oven or toasted.

Supplies

two 15 x 8-cm mini-loaf tins, cup, measuring jug and spoons, bowls, sieve, baking spatula or wooden spoon, plastic wrap, baking sheet, dinner knife

Ingredients

75 mL very warm (but not hot) water

2$\frac{1}{4}$ tsp quick-rise yeast

$\frac{1}{2}$ tsp golden granulated sugar

5 Tbsp (75 g) unsalted butter, cut into pieces

125 mL ($\frac{1}{2}$ cup) golden granulated sugar

5 Tbsp milk

2 large eggs

500 mL (2 cups) plain flour

4 Tbsp unsweetened cocoa powder

pinch of salt

1 Grease the mini-loaf tins.

2 Put the water, yeast and $\frac{1}{2}$ tsp sugar in a cup and jiggle to blend. Do not stir. Let stand at least 10 minutes to get foamy.

3 In a bowl, melt the butter at 50% power in the microwave (about 1 minute). Stir in the sugar and milk. Mix well and cool until barely warm. Mix in the eggs.

4 Into a big bowl, sift the flour, cocoa powder and salt. Mix well and add the butter mixture and foamy yeast. Use a baking spatula or wooden spoon to mix vigorously until the dough is smooth and stretchy. It will take at least 30 strong stirs. Cover the bowl with plastic wrap and leave in a warm spot to rise slightly (about 30 minutes).

5 Preheat oven to 350°F (180°C).

6 After the dough has risen, stir to pop large air bubbles. Use a baking spatula to scrape into the mini-loaf tins, gently pushing the dough to the edges. Place the tins on a baking sheet. Bake 40 to 45 minutes, until the tops of the bread are browned and firm. Cool until warm. Loosen the loaves with a dinner knife and tip out.

Makes 2 loaves Chocolate Bread.

Chocolate Bread

Cinnamon Rolls

Cinnamon Rolls

You'll feel like a master baker after you make these gorgeous soft buns oozing sweet caramel.

Supplies

20 x 20-cm square cake tin, plastic wrap,
8 hole muffin tin, cup, measuring jug and spoons,
bowls, whisk, baking spatula, wooden spoon, spoon,
dinner knife or bench scraper

Rolls

4 Tbsp very warm (but not hot) water

1 tsp quick-rise yeast

1 tsp golden granulated sugar

5 Tbsp milk

4 Tbsp (60 g) unsalted butter, cut into pieces

3 Tbsp skimmed milk powder

3 Tbsp golden granulated sugar

$1/4$ tsp vanilla extract

pinch of salt

1 large egg

425 mL ($1^3/4$ cups) plain flour

4 Tbsp plain flour

flour for dusting

Filling

5 Tbsp light muscovado brown sugar

4 Tbsp (60 g) unsalted butter, soft

$1/2$ tsp cinnamon, or more if you wish

pinch of salt

1   Line the square tin with plastic wrap, with lots of overhang up the sides. Grease the muffin tin.

2   To make the rolls, put the water, yeast and 1 tsp sugar in a measuring jug and jiggle to blend. Do not stir. Let stand at least 10 minutes to get foamy.

3   In a bowl, heat the milk and butter at 50% power in the microwave for about 2 minutes, or until the butter melts. Stir in the milk powder, 3 Tbsp sugar, vanilla and salt until dissolved. Cool to room temperature.

4   After the melted butter mixture has cooled, use a whisk to stir in the foamy yeast and the egg. Don't worry if this is lumpy. Switch to a baking spatula and gradually stir in 425 mL flour. Stir as hard as you can until the dough is smooth and stretchy. Cover the bowl with plastic wrap and set in a warm spot to rise 20 minutes.

5   In a small bowl, use a wooden spoon to cream the brown sugar, butter, cinnamon and salt. Set aside.

6   After the dough has risen, use a clean baking spatula or wooden spoon to mix in the 4 Tbsp flour. Use your hands to squeeze all the flour into the sticky dough. Cover with plastic wrap and let rise about 15 minutes.

7 Preheat oven to 325°F (160°C).

8 Flour your hands as needed and scoop the dough into the lined square tin. The dough will be sticky. Press out evenly to the edges of the tin, bursting any large air bubbles.

9 Use the back of a spoon to spread the filling on the dough. Keeping the dough in the tin, roll it into a cylinder, lifting the plastic and rolling as tightly as you can, without gaps. Use a dinner knife or a bench scraper dipped in flour to cut the dough into 8 equal slices. The dough is squishy, so don't worry about being too neat.

10 Put each slice (cut side up) into each hole of the greased muffin tin. Don't worry if the slices aren't round. As long
as you have the cut side up, they will bake into swirled rolls.

11 Bake about 25 minutes, or until the buns are golden. Cool slightly in the tins before unmolding onto a plate, with the caramel-covered bottoms on top. Drizzle with Sugar Glaze, if you wish.

Makes 8 Cinnamon Rolls.

Sugar Glaze for Cinnamon Rolls

4 Tbsp golden icing sugar

1$\frac{1}{2}$ Tbsp milk or cream, plus more if needed

Sift the icing sugar into a bowl. Mix in the milk or cream with a spoon. Drizzle over the warm cinnamon buns. Let stand a few minutes to set.

Cheddar Bread, Big Soft Pretzels

Cheddar Bread

This is a quick bread that works best if you use deep-coloured Cheddar instead of a pale one so you can see the cheese in the batter.

Supplies

20 x 10-cm loaf tin, small bowl or 500-mL glass measuring jug, measuring spoons, large bowl, sieve, fork, baking spatula, dinner knife

Ingredients

125 mL milk

5 Tbsp (75 g) unsalted butter, cut into pieces

500 mL (2 cups) plain flour

2 tsp baking powder

1$\frac{1}{2}$ tsp golden granulated sugar

1 tsp salt

2 large eggs

250 mL (1 cup) grated Cheddar

1 Preheat oven to 350°F (180°C).

2 Grease the loaf tin.

3 In a small bowl heat the milk and butter at 50% power in the microwave until the butter melts (about 2 minutes). Cool to room temperature.

4 Sift the flour, baking powder, salt and sugar into a large bowl and mix.

5 Use a fork to beat the eggs into the cooled milk mixture. Pour into the flour mixture. Use a baking spatula to stir until the batter is just moistened. Don't overmix. Stir in the grated Cheddar just enough to make streaks of grated cheese.

6 Scrape the batter into the greased tin. Bake about 45 minutes, or until the loaf is puffed, cracked on top and golden. Cool until warm. Loosen the bread from the tin with a dinner knife and tip out. Slice and eat while warm.

Makes 1 loaf Cheddar Bread.

Big Soft Pretzels

Chewy and tasty, these are especially delicious dipped in honey mustard.

Supplies

baking sheet, parchment paper, cup, measuring jug and spoons, large bowl, baking spatula or wooden spoon, damp cloth or paper towel, dinner knife or pizza cutter, pastry brush

Ingredients

150 mL very warm (but not hot) water

1 tsp golden granulated sugar

1/2 tsp quick-rise yeast

1 Tbsp olive oil

1/2 tsp fine sea salt (or table salt)

425 mL (1 3/4 cups) plain flour

4 Tbsp milk

1/4 tsp coarse salt

4 Tbsp coarsely grated Cheddar cheese

flour for dusting

honey mustard for dipping, if you wish

1   Line the baking sheet with parchment paper.

2   Put the water, sugar and yeast in a measuring jug and jiggle it to blend. Do not stir. Let stand at least 10 minutes to get foamy.

3   Pour the foamy yeast into a large bowl. Stir in the olive oil and fine salt (not the coarse salt). Gradually add the flour, stirring it in with a baking spatula or wooden spoon. When the dough is too stiff to stir, squeeze in the rest of the flour with your hands. Pull and squeeze the dough a few times, until it is smooth and stretchy.

4   Dust your work surface with flour. Put the dough on it. Cover with a damp cloth or paper towel and let it sit for 10 minutes.

5   Pat down the dough to about 2.5 cm thick. Use a dinner knife or pizza cutter to cut the dough into 7 equal pieces.

6   Preheat oven to 425°F (220°C).

7   Roll each piece of dough into a 1-cm thick rope about 38 cm long. The dough is springy, but keep rolling it. To make the pretzel shapes, overlap the ends of each rope, lay it on the lined sheet and shape into a wide circle, with the ends inside the circle.

8   Use a pastry brush to brush the pretzels with milk, then sprinkle with coarse salt and grated cheese. Bake 15 to 20 minutes, or until the pretzels are golden and the cheese is bubbling and crisp. Cool to lukewarm. Dip in honey mustard, if you wish.

Makes 7 Big Soft Pretzels.

One-Potato-Two Bread

This makes 2 puffy golden loaves of soft bread with a light potato flavour.
Just right for making little sandwiches.

Supplies

cup, measuring jug and spoons, bowls, baking spatula or wooden spoon, two 15 x 8-cm mini-loaf tins, plastic wrap, baking sheet, dinner knife

Ingredients

50 mL very warm (but not hot) water

1 tsp quick-rise yeast

1/2 tsp golden granulated sugar

175 mL milk

2 Tbsp unsalted butter

125 mL (1/2 cup) instant potato powder

1 large egg

375 mL (1 1/2 cups) plain flour

1 tsp salt

1 Put the water, yeast and sugar in a measuring jug and jiggle to blend. Do not stir. Let stand at least 10 minutes to get foamy.

2 In a bowl, heat the milk and butter at 50% power in the microwave until the butter melts (about 2 minutes). Use a baking spatula or wooden spoon to stir in the potato powder. Cool to lukewarm. Add the egg and yeast and stir until smooth.

3 In a large bowl, mix the flour and salt. Add the potato mixture and stir to make a sticky dough with no lumps. Cover the bowl with plastic wrap and set in a warm spot to rise for 30 minutes.

4 While the dough is rising, grease the loaf tins.

5 Use the baking spatula or wooden spoon to press out big air bubbles in the risen dough. Scrape into the tins, gently pressing the dough to the edges. Cover the tins with plastic wrap and let rise 15 minutes in the warm spot.

6 Preheat oven to 350°F (180°C).

7 Remove the plastic from the tins. Place tins on a baking sheet. Bake about 45 minutes, or until the breads are puffy and golden. Cool until warm. Loosen the loaves with a dinner knife and tip out.

Makes 2 loaves One-Potato-Two Bread.

One-Potato-Two Bread   Pizza Bread

9/10.

Pizza Bread

A moist, rib-sticking bread full of real pizza flavour.

Supplies *— 2lb loaf tin.*

20 x 10-cm loaf tin, bowls, measuring jug and spoons, sieve, baking spatula or wooden spoon, pizza cutter, whisk

Ingredients

500 mL (2 cups) plain flour

2 tsp baking powder

2 tsp dried oregano

1 tsp garlic salt

1 tsp golden granulated sugar

40 g pepperoni slices

125 mL tomato sauce (not tomato puree)

5 Tbsp grated Mozzarella or Cheddar cheese

4 Tbsp grated Parmesan cheese

4 Tbsp (60 g) unsalted butter, cut into pieces

150 mL milk

2 large eggs

1 Preheat oven to 350°F (180°C).

2 Grease the loaf tin.

3 Sift the flour and baking powder into a large bowl. Stir in the oregano, garlic salt and sugar. Set aside.

4 Use a pizza cutter to cut the pepperoni slices into small pieces. Mix with the tomato sauce and cheeses and set aside.

5 In another bowl, melt the butter at 50% power in the microwave (about 1 minute). Cool to lukewarm.

6 Use a whisk to mix the milk and eggs into the melted butter. Don't worry if bits of butter harden in the cold milk.

7 Pour the butter mixture into the flour mixture and stir until just moistened. Don't overmix.

8 Pour the pepperoni mixture on top and stir streaks through the batter. Don't mix in completely. Scrape the batter into the loaf tin. Spread it out evenly.

9 Bake 50 to 55 minutes, or until the top is puffed and golden.

Makes 1 loaf Pizza Bread.

Garlic Pepper Crisps

Even little children can make these crackers that crunch like crisps.
Use lemon pepper for the best taste.

Supplies

baking sheet, parchment paper, bowl, fork or small whisk, measuring spoons, pizza cutter or kitchen scissors, pastry brush

Ingredients

10 wonton wrappers (You won't need a whole package. Wrap tightly and freeze the rest.)

1 large egg white

1/2 tsp garlic salt

1/2 tsp onion salt

1/4 tsp lemon pepper or a pinch of black pepper

1/4 tsp dried parsley

1/8 tsp golden granulated sugar

2 Tbsp olive oil

1 heaped Tbsp grated Parmesan cheese

1 Tbsp sesame seeds, if you wish

1　Preheat oven to 350°F (180°C).

2　Line a baking sheet with parchment paper.

3　In a bowl, use a fork or small whisk to beat the egg white, salts, lemon pepper, dried parsley and sugar until no lumps are left. Set aside.

4　Lay the wonton wrappers on your work table. Use a pizza cutter or kitchen scissors to cut each wonton wrapper into quarters (4 squares). Lightly brush each square with olive oil on both sides.

5　Dip the pastry brush into the egg white mixture and generously dab each square. (The egg goes on only one side.) Sprinkle the egg side with grated cheese and sesame seeds, if you wish.

6　Carefully peel up the squares and lay them flat on the lined baking sheet, with the cheese side up. Bake 8 to 9 minutes, or until crisp and browned at the edges. Watch carefully in the last 2 minutes to avoid burning. Cool completely on the baking sheet.

Makes 40 Garlic Pepper Crisps.

Garlic Pepper Crisps

Split-Apart Wheat Crackers

Split-Apart Wheat Crackers

These aren't meant to be fancy. In fact, they look quite plain.
But they're just the thing to toss into a bowl of soup.

Supplies

baking sheet, parchment paper, bowls, measuring jug and spoons, sieve, pastry blender, cup, dinner knife, fork, rolling pin, pizza cutter

Ingredients

125 mL ($\frac{1}{2}$ cup) plain flour

4 Tbsp wholewheat flour

1 tsp golden granulated sugar

$\frac{1}{4}$ tsp bicarbonate of soda

$\frac{1}{4}$ tsp fine sea salt (or table salt)

2 Tbsp (30 g) unsalted butter, cold

2 Tbsp + 1 tsp milk

1 tsp lemon juice

$\frac{1}{2}$ tsp sesame seeds, if you wish

more salt for sprinkling, if you wish

1   Preheat oven to 400°F (200°C).

2   Line a baking sheet with parchment paper.

3   Into a large bowl, sift the plain and wholewheat flours, sugar, bicarbonate of soda and salt. (Be sure to add the bran left in the sieve.) Mix well.

4   Put the butter into the flour mixture and use a pastry blender to cut the dough into crumbs. Use a dinner knife to clean off the pastry blender as you work.

5   In a cup, mix the milk and lemon juice. Don't worry if the milk looks a bit curdled. Drizzle this over the crumbly flour mix. Stir with a fork until a stiff dough forms. If it is too dry to hold together, add a few more drops of milk. Use your hands to press all the crumbly bits into a ball of dough. Place on the lined baking sheet.

6   Use a rolling pin (you do not have to flour it) to roll the dough as thinly as you can, to about 3 mm. The dough puffs up a lot during baking. The thinner the dough, the crunchier the crackers. If using, sprinkle the sesame seeds and a little salt over the dough and roll them lightly with the rolling pin.

7   Use a pizza cutter to cut the dough into 2.5-cm strips, up and down and across, making small squares. Do not move the dough. The squares will puff and pull apart into little crackers during baking.

8   Bake 10 to 12 minutes, watching that the edges turn brown but don't burn. Take the crackers out of the oven to cool. (Leave the oven on.)

9   Break apart the crackers. Move the brown ones to the middle of the baking sheet and push the ones just turning golden to the edges. Return them to the oven for about 5 minutes, or until all the crackers are browned.

Makes several handfuls of Split-Apart Wheat Crackers.

3

Cookies

Butterscotchies   Coconut Macaroons   Oatmeal Raisin Cookies

Chocolate Two-Times　　　　　Chocolate Chip Cookies　　　　　Nutty Nuggets

Butterscotchies

Crisp, buttery cookies that are amazingly light, yet loaded with flavour.

Supplies

baking sheet, parchment paper, bowls, measuring jug and spoons, sieve, baking spatula or wooden spoon, tablespoon

Ingredients

5 Tbsp plain flour

1/4 tsp bicarbonate of soda

1/8 tsp salt

4 Tbsp light muscovado brown sugar

2 Tbsp (30 g) unsalted butter, soft

1 large egg yolk

5 Tbsp puffed rice cereal

2 Tbsp butterscotch chips (or chocolate chips, if you wish)

1 Preheat oven to 350°F (180°C).

2 Line a baking sheet with parchment paper.

3 Sift the flour, bicarbonate of soda and salt into a bowl and mix.

4 In another bowl, use a baking spatula or wooden spoon to cream the brown sugar and butter. Add the egg yolk. Mix well.

5 Gradually stir in the flour mixture. When it is well mixed, stir in the puffed rice cereal and butterscotch chips (or chocolate chips).

6 Use a tablespoon to drop the dough by level spoonfuls 5 cm apart on the lined baking sheet. Make 12 mounds. Bake 12 to 14 minutes, or until the cookies aren't shiny anymore and are golden brown. Cool completely on the sheet.

Makes 12 Butterscotchies.

Coconut Macaroons

The kitchen will fill with the scent of toasting coconut as these cookies bake.
They are very light and slightly chewy.

Supplies

baking sheet, parchment paper, large bowl, measuring spoons, 500-mL measuring jug or similar-sized bowl, rotary egg-beater, spoon, baking spatula

Ingredients

250 mL (1 cup) desiccated coconut

1 large egg white

1/8 tsp cream of tartar

sprinkle of salt

5 Tbsp golden granulated sugar

1 Preheat oven to 300°F (150°C).

2 Line a baking sheet with parchment paper.

3 Put the coconut in a large bowl. Set aside.

4 Put the egg white, cream of tartar and salt into a 500-mL measuring jug or similar-sized bowl. Beat with a rotary egg-beater until the egg white turns white and fluffy. Add the sugar a few heaped spoonfuls at a time, beating after you add.

5 Use a baking spatula to scrape the egg white into the coconut. Fold together. Drop by spoonfuls into mounds on the lined baking sheet, at least 8 cm apart. Make 10 mounds.

6 Bake 18 to 20 minutes, or until there's a little browning on the edges. Cool completely on the baking sheet before removing.

Makes 10 Coconut Macaroons.

Oatmeal Raisin Cookies

These wonderful cookies are crisp, not soft, and the toasted
rolled oats add crunch and a nutty taste.

Supplies

baking sheet, parchment paper, measuring jug and
spoons, bowls, sieve, baking spatula or wooden
spoon, teaspoon

Ingredients

155 mL (^{1}/$_2$ cup + 2 Tbsp) rolled oats
  (quick-cooking but not instant)

125 mL (^{1}/$_2$ cup) plain flour

^{1}/$_4$ tsp bicarbonate of soda

^{1}/$_8$ tsp cinnamon, if you wish

^{1}/$_8$ tsp salt

3 Tbsp (45 g) unsalted butter, soft

2 Tbsp light muscovado brown sugar

2 Tbsp golden granulated sugar

1 large egg

2–3 Tbsp raisins

1 Preheat oven to 350°F (180°C).

2 Line a baking sheet with parchment paper.

3 Spread the rolled oats on the parchment and toast
in the oven for about 10 minutes, or until the oats
are golden. Watch them carefully in the last
3 minutes so they don't scorch. Take them out of
the oven to cool, but keep the oven on.

4 Sift the flour, baking soda, cinnamon (if using) and
salt into a bowl and mix.

5 In another bowl, use a baking spatula or a wooden
spoon to cream the butter and the sugars. Add the
egg and mix well.

6 Gradually stir the flour mixture into the butter
mixture. Blend well. Stir in the toasted rolled oats
and raisins.

7 Be sure the baking sheet is completely cooled
before dropping teaspoons of the dough onto the
paper. Make 10 to 12 mounds at least 8 cm apart.

8 Bake 14 to 15 minutes, or until the cookies are
golden on top. Cool completely.

Makes 10–12 Oatmeal Raisin Cookies.

Chocolate Two-Times

You'll crave these crackle-top cookies that have chocolate chips studded in chocolate dough.

Supplies

baking sheet, parchment paper, bowl, measuring cups and spoons, large bowl or 1-L glass measuring jug, heatproof baking spatula, tablespoon

Ingredients

125 mL (1/2 cup) plain flour

4 Tbsp light muscovado brown sugar

2 Tbsp golden granulated sugar

1/8 tsp bicarbonate of soda

sprinkle of salt

4 squares semi-sweet chocolate (30 g each)

2 Tbsp (30 g) unsalted butter

1/2 tsp vanilla extract

1 large egg

4 Tbsp chocolate chips

1   Preheat oven to 350°F (180°C).

2   Line a baking sheet with parchment paper.

3   In a bowl, mix the flour, sugars, bicarbonate of soda and salt. Set aside. (It's important to pre-measure ingredients and have them ready to add to the melted chocolate before it cools.)

4   Melt the squares of chocolate and the butter in a bowl or 1-L glass measuring jug at 50% power in the microwave (about 3 1/2 minutes, stirring halfway).

5   Use a heatproof baking spatula to stir the vanilla into the melted chocolate. Gradually stir in the flour mixture. Add the egg and mix well. Stir in the chocolate chips.

6   Use a lightly greased tablespoon to scoop the dough and drop in mounds on the lined baking sheet. Make about 12 mounds, 5 cm apart.

7   Bake about 14 minutes, or until the edges are firm but the middle is still a little soft. Cool until lukewarm before removing from baking sheet.

Makes about 12 Chocolate Two-Times.

GOOD!

Chocolate Chip Cookies

Here's a small batch of the classic cookie to gobble up fresh. They stay deliciously soft.

Supplies

baking sheet, parchment paper, bowls, measuring jug and spoons, sieve, baking spatula or wooden spoon, tablespoon

Ingredients

165 mL ($^2/_3$ cup + 1 Tbsp) plain flour

$^1/_4$ tsp bicarbonate of soda

$^1/_8$ tsp salt

4 Tbsp (60 g) unsalted butter, soft

4 Tbsp light muscovado brown sugar

3 Tbsp golden granulated sugar

1 large egg yolk

$^1/_2$ tsp vanilla extract

1 Tbsp water

5 Tbsp semi-sweet chocolate chips

4 Tbsp coarsely chopped pecans or walnuts, if you wish (or chopped dried fruit or raisins)

1. Preheat oven to 350°F (180°C).

2. Line a baking sheet with parchment paper.

3. Sift the flour, bicarbonate of soda and salt into a bowl and mix.

4. In another bowl, use a baking spatula or wooden spoon to cream the butter and sugars. Add the egg yolk, vanilla and water. Mix well.

5. Gradually stir the flour mixture into the butter mixture. Stir in the chocolate chips and nuts, if using.

6. Use a tablespoon to scoop rounded spoonfuls of the cookie dough and drop mounds onto the lined baking sheet about 8 cm apart. Do not flatten.

7. Bake 10 to 12 minutes, or until the edges of the cookies begin to brown. Remove from oven and let the cookies cool on the baking sheet until they are firm, but still warm.

Makes about 12 Chocolate Chip Cookies.

Nutty Nuggets

These light-as-air cookies taste as good as they smell.
They're crisp at the edges and chewy in the middle.

Supplies

baking sheet, parchment paper, bowls, measuring jug and spoons, cup, small bowl, rotary egg-beater, spoon, baking spatula or wooden spoon

Ingredients

250 mL (1 cup) ground hazelnuts, ground almonds or pecans

2 Tbsp plain flour

2 Tbsp (30 g) unsalted butter

1 large egg

125 mL (1/2 cup) golden granulated sugar

1 or 2 drops of vanilla extract

1 Preheat oven to 350°F (180°C).

2 Line a baking sheet with parchment paper.

3 In a bowl, mix the ground nuts and the flour.

4 In a cup, melt the butter at 50% power in the microwave (about 30 seconds). Drizzle the melted butter over the nuts and flour. Mix well with a baking spatula or wooden spoon.

5 In a small bowl, use a rotary egg-beater to beat the egg until it is pale and thick, like thick cake batter. Gradually beat in heaping spoonfuls of the sugar and vanilla.

6 Pour the egg mixture into the bowl of ground nuts. Mix well with a baking spatula or wooden spoon. Drop by spoonfuls onto the lined baking sheet at least 8 cm apart. Make 15 mounds.

7 Bake about 15 minutes, or until the edges begin to turn golden and the tops are no longer shiny. Cool completely on the baking sheet before removing.

Makes 15 Nutty Nuggets.

Alphabet Cookies

Alphabet Cookies

Roll the dough into thin ropes, then shape into the letters of the alphabet, or Xs and Os to play a game.

baking sheet, parchment paper, bowl, measuring jug and spoons, sieve, heatproof baking spatula or wooden spoon, dinner knife

Ingredients

4 Tbsp (60 g) unsalted butter, cut into pieces

205 mL (3/4 cup + 2 Tbsp) plain flour

5 Tbsp golden icing sugar

sprinkle of salt

2 Tbsp corn syrup (preferably light variety)

1/4 tsp vanilla extract

1 large egg yolk

flour for dusting

1 Preheat oven to 325°F (160°C).

2 Line a baking sheet with parchment paper.

3 In a bowl, melt the butter at 50% power in a microwave (about 30 seconds). Cool.

4 Sift the flour, icing sugar and salt into a bowl and mix. Set aside.

5 Use a heatproof baking spatula or wooden spoon to stir the corn syrup and vanilla into the melted butter until smooth. Add the egg yolk and mix well.

6 Pour the butter mixture into the flour mixture. Blend well. Keeping the dough in the bowl, use your hands to knead and squeeze the dough. It might be crumbly at first, but knead until it is smooth.

7 Lightly dust your work table with flour. Roll pieces of dough into 1-cm thick ropes and bend them into letters. Or, to make an Xs and Os game, use a dinner knife to cut the dough into 12 equal pieces. Roll each piece into a 1-cm thick rope. Make Os by looping the ropes into circles and pinching the ends together. Make Xs by cutting each rope in half, crossing the pieces and pressing down to overlap them. Place the cookies at least 2.5 cm apart on the lined baking sheet.

8 Bake 10 to 12 minutes, or until the edges begin to turn golden. Cool completely on the baking sheet before painting with Alphabet Icing.

Makes an assortment of Alphabet Cookies.

Alphabet Icing

250 mL (1 cup) golden icing sugar

1 Tbsp milk (or more to thin)

1/2 tsp lemon juice

assorted natural food colourings

Sift the icing sugar into a small bowl. Stir in the milk and lemon juice until smooth. Add a few drops more milk to thin, if needed.

Pour into small dishes and tint with food colourings as you wish. To tint a small amount of icing, dip toothpicks into colourings and stir through. Use a small brush to paint the icing onto the cooled cookies. Let icing dry to harden.

Alphabet Cookies (Xs and Os)   Almond Thumbprints, Shortbread Domes

Almond Thumbprints

Top these either with a whole almond or dollop of jam.

baking sheet, parchment paper, bowls, measuring jug and spoons, sieve, baking spatula or wooden spoon

Ingredients

5 Tbsp plain flour

4 Tbsp golden icing sugar

125 mL ($\frac{1}{2}$ cup) ground almonds

$\frac{1}{4}$ tsp baking powder

$\frac{1}{8}$ tsp salt

3 Tbsp (45 g) unsalted butter, soft

2 Tbsp golden granulated sugar

1 large egg yolk

$\frac{1}{4}$ tsp vanilla extract

20 blanched whole almonds or about
   4 Tbsp jam

1. Line a baking sheet with parchment paper.

2. Sift the flour and icing sugar into a bowl. Mix in the ground almonds, baking powder and salt.

3. In another bowl, use a baking spatula or wooden spoon to cream the butter and sugar. Mix in the egg yolk and vanilla.

4. Gradually stir the flour mixture into the butter mixture. When the dough gets too stiff to stir, use your hands to knead in the rest of the flour mixture to make a soft dough. If the dough is too sticky, knead in another teaspoon of flour.

5. Preheat oven to 325°F (160°C).

6. Pinch off pieces about a $\frac{1}{2}$ tablespoon each. Roll each piece of dough into a ball. This might seem like a small amount of dough, but it's just right for small cookies because the dough rises a lot as it bakes. Place the balls about 5 cm apart on the lined baking sheet. Press your thumb or finger into the middle of each ball to make a dent in the middle. Fill the dents either with an almond or a little jam. Chill the sheet of cookies 10 minutes.

7. Bake cookies about 12 minutes, or until the edges turn lightly golden. Cool completely on the baking sheet before removing.

Makes about 20 Almond Thumbprints.

Shortbread Domes

A melt-in-your-mouth shortbread rolled in sprinkles before baking.

Supplies

baking sheet, parchment paper, small dishes, measuring jug and spoons, bowls, baking spatula or wooden spoon

Ingredients

205 mL (3/4 cup + 2 Tbsp) plain flour

3 Tbsp cornflour

115 g unsalted butter, soft

4 Tbsp golden granulated sugar

assorted sprinkles and coloured sugars for decorating

1 Line a baking sheet with parchment paper. Pour sprinkles into small dishes. Set aside.

2 In a bowl, mix together the flour and cornflour.

3 In another bowl, use a baking spatula or wooden spoon to cream the butter and sugar. Gradually stir in the flour mixture to make a soft dough. Squeeze any loose crumbs into the dough.

4 Pinch off a walnut-sized blob of dough and and roll it into a 2.5-cm ball. Gently press the top half of it into the sprinkles. Try not to flatten the ball as you press down. Roll each ball and dip it in the sprinkles before rolling the next one. You'll get about 14 balls.

5 Place balls 5 cm apart on the lined baking sheet with the sprinkles facing up.

6 Preheat oven to 300°F (150°C).

7 Bake for about 22 minutes, or until the tops of the cookies are firm when gently pressed. They should be lightly golden around the edges. Cool completely on the baking sheet before removing.

Makes about 14 Shortbread Domes.

Chocolate-Mint Pinwheel Lollies

This recipe looks long, but it's really just splitting 1 bowl of batter into 2 doughs. Follow the steps to make 2-toned cookies baked on wooden sticks like lollipops.

Supplies

20 x 20-cm tin, plastic wrap, baking sheet, parchment paper, bowls, measuring jug and spoons, baking spatula or wooden spoon, dinner knife, about 18 wooden lolly sticks

Butter Mixture

225 g unsalted butter, soft
250 mL (1 cup) golden granulated sugar
1 large egg
3 Tbsp corn syrup
$\frac{1}{2}$ tsp bicarbonate of soda
$\frac{1}{8}$ tsp salt
flour for dusting

Mint Dough

200 mL Butter Mixture
1 tsp peppermint extract
about 8 drops of natural green food colouring
300 mL (1$\frac{1}{4}$ cups) plain flour

Chocolate Dough

rest of Butter Mix
1 tsp vanilla extract
4 Tbsp unsweetened cocoa powder
400 mL (1$\frac{2}{3}$ cups) plain flour

1 Line the square tin with plastic wrap and lots of overhang. Line a baking sheet with parchment paper.

2 To make the Butter Mixture, in a large bowl, use a baking spatula or wooden spoon to cream the butter and sugar. Add the egg, corn syrup, bicarbonate of soda and salt. Mix well.

3 To make the Mint Dough, measure out 200 mL of Butter Mixture into another large bowl and add a drop of green food colouring to it so you won't have a mix-up. (Don't mix up the two bowls of Butter Mixture because they are different amounts.) Set aside.

4 To make the Chocolate Dough, use the Butter Mixture in the bowl that does not have the food colouring. Add the vanilla and cocoa powder. Mix well. Gradually stir in 400 mL (1$\frac{2}{3}$ cups) flour. When the dough gets too stiff, use your hands to knead it into a smooth ball, working inside the bowl. If the dough is too sticky, knead in a teaspoon of flour.

5 Pinch off and drop big blobs of the Chocolate Dough into the lined pan. Press them down to cover the bottom of the pan in a thin layer. Dust hands with flour, if needed. Chill the pan for about 10 minutes. (Don't leave it for much longer or it will get too stiff to roll.) Wash your hands.

continued >>

Chocolate-Mint Pinwheel Lollies

6   While the Chocolate Dough chills, finish making the Mint Dough. Stir the peppermint extract and another seven drops of green food colouring into the Butter Mixture for a bright colour. Mix well. Gradually stir in 300 mL (1 1/4 cups) flour. When the dough gets too stiff, use your hands to knead it into a smooth ball, working inside the bowl. The dough might seem crumbly at first, but keep squeezing and it will soften.

7   After chilling the Chocolate Dough, drop blobs of Mint Dough on top and press to cover the Chocolate Dough. Dust hands with flour, if needed.

8   Use the plastic to lift the square of dough out of the tin and onto your work table. Keep the plastic under the dough. To make it easy to roll, use the heels of your hands to flatten one side of the dough to 5 mm thick. (Flatten 5 cm into the slab.) Place this flattened strip in front of you to begin rolling. Lift the plastic to help you roll the dough into a tight cylinder. Pat the ends in. Wrap the dough in the plastic. If the cylinder is fatter in some parts than others, roll the fatter parts a few times to even it out. You should have a cylinder that is 6 cm in diameter. Chill 30 minutes.

9   Preheat oven to 350°F (180°C).

10 After chilling, remove the plastic, then use a dinner knife to cut the cylinder into 1-cm thick rounds. Or a grown-up can cut it with a sharp knife. If the dough is too stiff to cut, let it warm up a little first. Place the rounds on the lined baking sheet at least 8 cm apart.

11 Insert wooden sticks into the rounds so they look like lollipops. Pat the rounds back into circles if they get squished.

12 Bake the cookies about 16 minutes, or until the edges are firm, the tops are no longer shiny and the green dough is still green. (If baked too long, the green dough will turn golden.) They might be slightly soft in the middle, but will firm up once cooled. Cool completely on the sheet.

Makes about 20 Chocolate-Mint Pinwheel Lollies.

Gingerbread Men

Ideal for the holidays. Decorating is easy. Brush Alphabet Icing (page 69) on the baked ginger-bread men and decorate with candy eyes and buttons. Mouths are drawn with food colouring.

Supplies

baking sheet, parchment paper, bowls, measuring jug and spoons, baking spatula or wooden spoon, rolling pin, 8-cm gingerbread man shaped pastry cutter, small paint brush, toothpicks

Ingredients

500 mL (2 cups) plain flour

1 tsp cinnamon

1/2 tsp bicarbonate of soda

1/2 tsp ground ginger

1/4 tsp nutmeg

1/8 tsp allspice or ground cloves

1/8 tsp salt

5 Tbsp (75 g) unsalted butter, soft

4 Tbsp molasses

1 large egg yolk

2 Tbsp light muscovado brown sugar

2 Tbsp golden granulated sugar

1 Tbsp milk

1 tsp corn syrup

flour for dusting

sugar sprinkles, dragees and cake decorations for eyes and buttons

natural food colouring for mouths

1 Cut 2 sheets of parchment paper the size of your baking sheet. Put one piece on the baking sheet.

2 In a bowl, mix the flour, cinnamon, bicarbonate of soda, ginger, nutmeg, allspice or cloves and salt.

3 In another bowl, use a baking spatula or wooden spoon to mix the butter, molasses, egg yolk, brown and golden sugars, milk and corn syrup well.

4 Gradually stir the flour mixture into the butter mixture. When the dough gets too stiff to stir, use your hands to knead in the rest of the flour mixture until you have a smooth dough.

5 Dust the parchment on the baking sheet with flour. Flour your hands and scoop the dough onto the dusted paper. Gently press to form a slab of dough about 2.5 cm thick. Chill 20 minutes.

6 Preheat oven to 350°F (180°C).

7 Slide the chilled dough (still on the paper) onto your work table. Lightly dust the top of the dough with flour. Put the second piece of paper on top. Put your rolling pin on the top paper and roll the dough to just under 5 mm thick. Lift the top paper to check that the dough isn't sticking. If it is, lightly dust with more flour before rolling again. Remove the top paper. Cut the dough with the pastry cutter.

8   Put the top paper on the baking sheet (clean side up). Place figures at least 5 cm apart. Chill about 10 minutes before baking.

9   Bake about 10 minutes, or until they are no longer shiny on top. Cool completely on the baking sheet before removing. The gingerbread men will firm up as they cool. Re-roll dough scraps, cut, chill and bake in batches.

10 After cooling, paint tops with Alphabet Icing (page 69). Place sprinkles, dragees or decorations for eyes and buttons. Let the icing harden. Dip the tip of a toothpick in food colouring and draw mouths. Let dry.

Makes about 18 Gingerbread Men.

Vanilla Satins, Chocolate Satins, Alphabet Icing, Cookie Fillings

Chocolate Satins

This dough is ideal for cookie cutters because it holds its shape well. Delicious plain or sandwiched with cookie fillings (page 81). If filling, use only 1 cookie cutter shape.

(page 81)

Supplies

baking sheet, parchment paper, bowls, measuring jug and spoons, baking spatula or wooden spoon, rolling pin, cookie cutters about 5 cm wide

Ingredients

190 mL (³⁄₄ cup + 1 Tbsp) plain flour
2 Tbsp unsweetened cocoa powder
¹⁄₄ tsp bicarbonate of soda
5 Tbsp (75 g) unsalted butter, soft
4 Tbsp golden caster sugar
1 large egg yolk
¹⁄₂ Tbsp corn syrup
¹⁄₄ tsp vanilla extract
flour for dusting

1 Cut 2 sheets of parchment paper the size of your baking sheet. Put one piece on the baking sheet.

2 Mix the flour, cocoa powder and bicarbonate of soda in a bowl. Set aside.

3 In another bowl, use a baking spatula or wooden spoon to cream the butter and sugar. Stir in the egg yolk, corn syrup and vanilla. Mix until smooth.

4 Gradually stir the flour mixture into the butter mixture. When the dough gets too stiff to stir, use your hands to knead the rest of the flour mixture into the dough, keeping it in the bowl.

5 Dust the parchment on the baking sheet with flour. Flour your hands and scoop the dough onto the dusted paper. Gently press to form a slab about 2.5 cm thick. Chill 20 minutes.

6 Preheat oven to 350°F (180°C).

7 Slide the chilled dough (still on the paper) onto your work table. Lightly dust the top of the dough with flour. Put the second piece of paper on top of the dough. Put your rolling pin on the top paper and roll the dough to just under 5 mm thick. Lift the top paper to check that the dough isn't sticking. If it is, lightly dust with more flour before rolling again. Remove the top paper. Cut the dough with cookie cutters about 5 cm wide.

8 Put the top paper on the baking sheet (clean side up). Place cookies at least 5 cm apart. Chill 10 minutes before baking.

9 Bake 12 to 14 minutes, or until the cookies are no longer shiny on top. Cool completely on the baking sheet before removing. Re-roll dough scraps, cut, chill and bake in batches.

Makes about 24 Chocolate Satins.

Vanilla Satins

Don't be fooled by how plain these look. They're simply delicious and perfect for decorating. Paint with Alphabet Icing (page 69) or sandwich with a cookie filling (page 81).

Supplies

baking sheet, parchment paper, bowls, measuring jug and spoons, sieve, baking spatula or wooden spoon, rolling pin, cookie cutters about 4 cm wide

Ingredients

175 mL (¾ cup) plain flour

4 Tbsp (60 g) unsalted butter, soft

1 Tbsp cream cheese, soft

4 Tbsp golden granulated sugar

1 egg yolk

½ tsp vanilla extract

flour for dusting

1. Cut 2 sheets of parchment paper the size of your baking sheet. Put one piece on the baking sheet.

2. Sift the flour into a bowl. Set aside.

3. In another bowl, use a baking spatula or wooden spoon to cream the butter, cream cheese and sugar until well mixed. Stir in the egg yolk and vanilla. Mix well.

4. Gradually stir in the flour. When the dough gets too stiff to stir, use your hands to knead in the rest of the flour to make a soft dough. (Knead it inside the bowl.)

5. Dust the parchment on the baking sheet with flour. Flour your hands and scoop the dough onto the dusted paper. Gently press to form a slab about 2.5 cm thick. Chill 20 minutes.

6. Preheat oven to 350°F (180°C).

7. Slide the chilled dough (still on the paper) onto your work table. Lightly dust the top of the dough with flour. Put the second piece of paper on top of the dough. Put your rolling pin on the top paper and roll the dough to just under 5 mm thick. Lift the top paper to check that the dough isn't sticking. If it is, lightly dust with more flour before rolling again. Remove the top paper. Cut the dough with cookie cutters about 4 cm wide.

8. Put the top paper on the baking sheet (clean side up). Place cookies at least 5 cm apart. Chill 10 minutes before baking.

9. Bake 10 to 12 minutes, or until the cookies are no longer shiny on top. The cookies should stay pale yellow. Do not let them turn golden. Cool completely on the baking sheet before removing. Re-roll dough scraps, cut, chill and bake in batches.

Makes about 24 Vanilla Satins.

Cookie Fillings

Each recipe will fill 12 pairs of Satin cookies.

Coconut Cookie Filling

125 mL ($\frac{1}{2}$ cup) desiccated coconut

5 Tbsp sweetened condensed milk

2 tsp golden icing sugar

Mix ingredients in a small bowl. Spread thinly on about 12 Vanilla or Chocolate Satins. Gently press a second cookie on top.

Milk Chocolate Cookie Filling

150 mL ($\frac{2}{3}$ cup) golden icing sugar

5 Tbsp sweetened condensed milk

1 Tbsp unsalted butter, soft

1 Tbsp unsweetened cocoa powder

$\frac{1}{4}$ tsp vanilla extract

Mix ingredients in a small bowl. Spread thinly on about 12 Vanilla or Chocolate Satins. Gently press a second cookie on top.

Caramel Cookie Filling

150 mL ($\frac{2}{3}$ cup) light muscovado brown sugar

4 Tbsp sweetened condensed milk

1 Tbsp unsalted butter, soft

1 Tbsp corn syrup

$\frac{1}{2}$ tsp vanilla extract

Use a heatproof baking spatula to mix the ingredients in a bowl until smooth. Heat at 50% power in the microwave for 2 minutes. Stir with the baking spatula. Heat again at 50% power for about 1 minute, until bubbly and thickened and the brown sugar is melted. Cool until barely warm before filling cookies. Use a dinner knife or small palette knife to spread the caramel. Gently press a second cookie on top.

PB&Js

Peanut butter and jam cookies that look like tiny slices of bread smeared with jam. Be sure to use only peanut butter made from 100% peanuts, with no other ingredients listed on the jar.

Supplies

15 x 8-cm mini-loaf tin, plastic wrap, baking sheet, parchment paper, bowls, measuring jug and spoons, baking spatula or wooden spoon, dinner knife

Ingredients

125 mL ($1/2$ cup) creamy peanut butter (use peanut butter made from 100% peanuts)

4 Tbsp (60 g) unsalted butter, soft

1 large egg

1 Tbsp corn syrup

300 mL ($1^1/4$ cups) plain flour

250 mL (1 cup) golden icing sugar

$1/4$ tsp bicarbonate of soda

sprinkle of salt

about 3 Tbsp raspberry or strawberry jam

1 Line the mini-loaf tin with plastic wrap, leaving lots of overhang. Line a baking sheet with parchment paper.

2 In a bowl, use a baking spatula or wooden spoon to cream the peanut butter and butter until well blended. Mix in the egg and corn syrup.

3 In another bowl, mix the flour, icing sugar, bicarbonate of soda and salt. Gradually stir into the peanut butter mixture. When the dough gets too stiff to stir, use your hands to knead in the rest of the flour mix. (Keep the dough in the bowl.)

4 Press the dough firmly into the lined tin. Chill at least 30 minutes.

5 Lift the chilled dough out of the tin in one piece. It will be in the shape of the loaf tin. Use a dinner knife to cut the loaf in half lengthwise. You will have 2 long, skinny "loaves." Cut into slices no thicker than 5 mm thick. Don't worry if some dough crumbles as you cut. Pat it back into place.

6 Leave the slices as they are or shape them into little bread slices. To shape, lay the dough slices flat on the lined baking sheet about 5 cm apart. Pat the top corners of the slices to round them. About $1/3$ of the way down from the top, pinch notches into sides.

7 Preheat oven to 325°F (160°C).

8 Thickly smear each slice with jam. Chill 10 minutes.

9 Bake the cookies 15 to 17 minutes, or until the edges are browned. Cool completely on the baking sheet before removing.

Makes about 28 PB&Js.

Rainbow Sugar Cookies

You don't have to tint these cookies, but it's lots of fun rolling the colours together. If you make them without food colouring, ice them with one of the cake icings (pages 91–92) and have fun scattering sugar sprinkles over top.

Supplies

baking sheet, parchment paper, bowls, measuring jug and spoons, sieve, baking spatula or wooden spoon, 2 spoons, rolling pin, pastry cutter about 5 cm wide

Single Batch

325 mL (1$\frac{1}{3}$ cups) plain flour

$\frac{1}{2}$ tsp baking powder

pinch of salt

125 mL ($\frac{1}{2}$ cup) golden granulated sugar

4 Tbsp unsalted butter, soft

1 large egg

1$\frac{1}{2}$ tsp milk

$\frac{1}{4}$ tsp vanilla extract

2 different natural food colourings

flour for dusting

1   Cut 2 sheets of parchment paper the size of your baking sheet. Put one piece on the baking sheet.

2   Sift the flour, baking powder and salt into a bowl and mix.

3   In another bowl, use a baking spatula or wooden spoon to cream the sugar and butter. Mix in the egg, milk and vanilla. Scrape into the flour mixture and stir to make a soft dough. Squeeze any loose crumbs into the dough.

4   Divide the dough into 3 roughly equal portions and put them in separate bowls. Leave one of the doughs uncoloured, but add a few drops of food colouring to the other doughs. Use separate spoons to mix in the colourings.

5   Dust the parchment paper on the baking sheet with flour. Pinch off walnut-sized blobs of the doughs and randomly drop them on the lined baking sheet. Flour your hands and gently press the blobs until they form a slab about 2.5 cm thick. Make sure there are no holes. Chill 30 minutes.

6   Preheat oven to 350°F (180°C).

7   Slide the chilled dough (still on the paper) onto your work table. Lightly dust the top of the dough with flour. Put the second piece of paper on top of the dough. Put your rolling pin on the top paper and roll the dough to just under 5 mm thick. Lift the top paper to check that the dough isn't sticking. If it is, lightly dust with more flour. Remove the top paper. Cut the dough with pastry cutters about 5 cm wide.

8   Put the top paper on the baking sheet (clean side up). Place cookies at least 5 cm apart. Bake 13 to 15 minutes, or until the cookies are no longer shiny on top. Cool completely on the baking sheet before removing. Gather dough scraps together and chill dough again once it is too soft to work. Roll, cut and bake in batches.

Makes about 24 Rainbow Sugar Cookies.

Double Batch of Rainbow Sugar Cookies

These make great cookies for parties and holidays so here is the ingredient list for twice as many cookies. Follow the steps for a single batch.

650 mL (2²/₃ cups) plain flour

1 tsp baking powder

pinch of salt

250 mL (1 cup) golden granulated sugar

115 g unsalted butter, soft

2 large eggs

1 Tbsp milk

¹/₂ tsp vanilla extract

2 different natural food colourings

flour for dusting

Makes about 48 Rainbow Sugar Cookies.

4

Cakes

Classic Little Vanilla Cake

A buttery vanilla cake in 2 sizes. Choose 1 set of ingredients, but
follow the same method for both.

Supplies
15-cm round white ceramic souffle dish or 20-cm
round metal cake tin, parchment or wax paper, bowls,
measuring jug and spoons, sieve, baking spatula or
wooden spoon, whisk, dinner knife, plate

15-cm Dish
175 mL ($^3/_4$ cup) plain flour
$1^1/_2$ tsp baking powder
sprinkle of salt
125 mL ($^1/_2$ cup) golden granulated sugar
4 Tbsp (60 g) unsalted butter, soft
1 large egg
$^1/_2$ tsp vanilla extract
125 mL milk

OR

20-cm Tin
265 mL (1 cup + 1 Tbsp) plain flour
2 tsp baking powder
sprinkle of salt
175 mL ($^3/_4$ cup) golden granulated sugar
5 Tbsp (75 g) unsalted butter, soft
1 large egg
1 tsp vanilla extract
150 mL milk

1. Preheat oven to 350°F (180°C).

2. Grease and flour the sides of the souffle dish or
   cake tin. Line the bottom with a round of parchment or wax paper.

3. Sift the flour, baking powder and salt into a bowl
   and mix.

4. In another bowl, use a baking spatula or wooden
   spoon to cream the sugar and butter. Blend in the
   egg and vanilla.

5. Switch to a whisk to gradually stir in the milk. Stir
   in spoonfuls of the flour mixture until you have a
   smooth batter.

6. Use the spatula to scrape the batter into the cake tin,
   spreading evenly. **For the 15-cm size,** bake 35 to 40
   minutes or until the top of the cake is pale golden
   and a skewer inserted into the middle comes out
   clean. **For the 20-cm size,** bake 40 to 45 minutes.
   Cool completely.

7. To unmold the cake, run a dinner knife twice around
   the edge. Get help to tip the cake out. Peel off the
   parchment paper, if you wish. (If you keep the paper
   on, it is easier to slide the cake onto a plate or rack,
   but remember not to slice through the paper when
   cutting the cake for eating.) Set right-side-up on a
   plate ready to frost.

Makes 1 Classic Little Vanilla Cake.

Devon Cream Pie Drizzle

This chocolate drizzle helps turn a 15-cm Classic Little Vanilla Cake (page 88) into a chilled dessert. Not recommended for 20-cm round cakes.

Supplies

bowl, measuring jug and spoons, sieve, cup, stirring spoons, baking spatula, dinner knife, plate

Ingredients

250 mL (1 cup) golden icing sugar

2 Tbsp unsweetened cocoa powder

sprinkle of salt

2 Tbsp water

1 Tbsp (15 g) unsalted butter

1/4 tsp vanilla extract

1 Classic Little Vanilla Cake (15-cm round)

125 mL soft vanilla custard (ready made)

1 Sift the icing sugar, cocoa powder and salt into a bowl and mix.

2 In a cup, heat the water and butter at 50% power in the microwave until the butter is melted (about 30 seconds). Stir in the vanilla. Pour into the bowl of icing sugar and cocoa. Mix smooth with a baking spatula.

3 Get help slicing the cake in half cross-wise. If you keep the paper on, it is easier to slide the cake from a baking rack to a plate, but remember not to slice through the paper when cutting the cake for eating.

4 Place the bottom half of the cake on a baking rack. Use a dinner knife to spread the top of it with the custard. Replace the top of the cake. Spoon the drizzle over the top, letting it drip over the sides. Let the drizzle harden before sliding the cake onto a plate. Chill before slicing.

Makes 1 Devon Cream Pie.

Devon Cream Pie

Classic Little Vanilla Cake

Cake Icings

Any of the recipes on these pages will ice and fill a 15-cm cake or ice a 20-cm round or square cake (not filled). Also try Chocolate Cream Icing (page 101)

Easiest Icing

Whipping cream makes this an easy recipe. Tint it a pretty pale colour. This is a slightly thicker version of Tea Party Icing (page 98).

Supplies

bowls, measuring jug and spoons, sieve, small bowl or 500-mL measuring jug, rotary egg-beater, baking spatula, whisk

Ingredients

500 mL (2 cups) golden icing sugar

175 mL whipping cream

sprinkle of salt

drop of vanilla extract

drop of natural food colouring

Sift the icing sugar into a bowl. Set aside.

In a small bowl or 500-mL measuring jug, use a rotary egg-beater to beat the cream and salt until fluffy. Scrape into a bowl. Use a whisk to stir in spoonfuls of the icing sugar until smooth and fluffy. Stir in the vanilla and food colouring. Add a spoonful more icing sugar to thicken or a few drops of cream to thin, if needed.

Easiest Chocolate Icing

There's cocoa powder in this version to give it a chocolate taste.

Supplies

bowls, measuring jug and spoons, sifter, small bowl or 500-mL measuring jug, rotary egg-beater, baking spatula, whisk

Ingredients

500 mL (2 cups) golden icing sugar

1 Tbsp unsweetened cocoa powder

175 mL whipping cream

sprinkle of salt

drop of vanilla extract

Sift the icing sugar and cocoa powder into a bowl and mix. Set aside.

In a small bowl or 500-mL measuring jug, use a rotary egg-beater to beat the cream and salt until fluffy. Scrape into a bowl. Use a whisk to stir in spoonfuls of the icing sugar mixture until smooth and fluffy. Stir in the vanilla. Add a spoonful more icing sugar to thicken or a few drops of cream to thin, if needed.

Buttercream Icing

The softer your butter, the smoother this icing will be. This rich icing is best for tinting brighter colours.

Supplies

bowls, measuring jug and spoons, sieve, baking spatula or wooden spoon

Ingredients

625 mL (2$\frac{1}{2}$ cups) golden icing sugar

4 Tbsp (60 g) unsalted butter, soft

4 Tbsp milk or cream (or more to thin)

1 tsp vanilla or other extract flavour

a few drops of natural food colouring, if you wish

Sift the icing sugar into a bowl. Set aside.

In another bowl, use a baking spatula or wooden spoon to cream the butter until it is very soft. Gradually stir in a few spoonfuls of the icing sugar. Mix in the milk or cream. Stir in the rest of the icing sugar.

Stir in the extract and food colouring, if using. Add a spoonful more icing sugar to thicken or a few drops of milk or cream to thin, if the frosting is too stiff.

Dark Chocolate Icing

This icing stays soft and glossy.

Supplies

bowl, measuring jug and spoons, heatproof baking spatula

Ingredients

250 mL (1 cup) semi-sweet chocolate chips

5 Tbsp sour cream

2 drops of vanilla extract

Put the chocolate chips in a bowl and microwave at 50% power for 1$\frac{1}{2}$ minutes. Stir with the heatproof baking spatula. Heat again on 50% power for another minute, until melted. Stir in the sour cream and vanilla until smooth.

How to Ice a Cake

1 To keep icing off your cake plate, cut 4 straight strips of parchment or wax paper that are longer than the cake. Each strip should be about 5 cm wide. Put your cake on your plate and slip the paper strips partly under the edges of the cake.

2 You may or may not want to fill a cake. To fill a cake means to cut it in half across the middle and spread icing on the bottom layer before replacing the top. This works well with 15-cm cakes. Filling is not recommended for 20-cm round or square cakes because the layers are large and can wobble and split when picked up.

To fill a 15-cm cake, get help slicing the cake in half. Scoop a blob of icing onto the bottom half. It is easier to start with too much icing than too little so the cake crumbs won't rub up as you spread the icing. Use a small baking spatula or palette knife to spread icing evenly over the edges. Put the top back on.

3 For both filled and unfilled cakes, simply scoop a big blob of icing onto the top and spread it over the top and sides. Remember, it does not have to be perfect. It will always be delicious. Younger kids may find it easier to ice only the top of a cake, leaving the sides plain. This looks nice, too.

4 When you are happy with your icing job, decorate with sprinkles or other cake decorations, if you wish. Carefully pull out the paper strips.

Easiest Chocolate Cake

Easiest Chocolate Cake

This lovely butterless chocolate cake bakes to a slightly craggy top that can be glazed or iced. This recipe is offered in 2 sizes. Choose 1 set of ingredients, but follow the same method for both.

Supplies

15-cm round white ceramic souffle dish or 20-cm round metal cake tin, parchment or wax paper, sieve, baking spatula, whisk, bowls, measuring jug and spoons, dinner knife, baking rack

15-cm Dish

150 mL ($\frac{2}{3}$ cup) plain flour

5 Tbsp unsweetened cocoa powder

$\frac{1}{4}$ tsp baking powder

$\frac{1}{4}$ tsp bicarbonate of soda

sprinkle of salt

140 mL ($\frac{1}{2}$ cup + 1 Tbsp) golden granulated sugar

2 Tbsp vegetable oil

1 tsp vanilla extract

1 large egg

150 mL milk

OR

20-cm Tin

250 mL (1 cup) plain flour

125 mL ($\frac{1}{2}$ cup) unsweetened cocoa powder

$\frac{1}{2}$ tsp baking powder

$\frac{1}{4}$ tsp bicarbonate of soda

sprinkle of salt

1 large egg

175 mL ($\frac{3}{4}$ cup) golden granulated sugar

4 Tbsp vegetable oil

2 tsp vanilla extract

175 mL milk

1 Preheat oven to 350°F (180°C).

2 Grease and flour the sides of the souffle dish or cake tin. Line the bottom with a round of parchment or wax paper.

3 Sift the flour, cocoa powder, baking powder, bicarbonate of soda and salt into a bowl and mix.

4 In another bowl, use a whisk to stir the egg, sugar, vegetable oil and vanilla until smooth.

5 Still using the whisk, stir spoonfuls of the flour mixture and splashes of the milk — switching between the two — into the sugar mix. Stir until smooth.

6 Use a baking spatula to scrape the batter into the cake tin. **For the 15-cm size,** bake about 45 minutes, until a skewer inserted into the middle comes out clean. **For the 20-cm size,** bake about 50 minutes. Cool completely.

7 To unmold the cake, run a dinner knife twice around the edge. Get help to tip the cake out. Set right-side-up on a baking rack to glaze, if you wish. Use Milk Chocolate Glaze (page 96), Boston Cream Pie Drizzle (page 89) or one of the cake icings (pages 91–92).

Makes 1 Easiest Chocolate Cake.

Milk Chocolate Glaze

Supplies

bowls, measuring jug and spoons, sieve, baking
spatula or wooden spoon

Ingredients

125 mL ($^1/_2$ cup) golden icing sugar

1 Tbsp unsweetened cocoa powder

1 Tbsp (15 g) unsalted butter, soft

4 Tbsp sweetened condensed milk

$^1/_4$ tsp vanilla extract

a few drops of milk (to thin, if needed)

Sift and mix the icing sugar and cocoa powder in a
bowl.

In another bowl, use a baking spatula or wooden spoon
to cream the butter. Gradually mix in the condensed milk
and vanilla until smooth. Stir in spoonfuls of the icing
sugar mixture. Stir until smooth. It will be very thick. If
you would like it thinner, add a few drops of milk.

Spoon or spread over the cake, letting the glaze drip
down the sides.

Tea Party Vanilla Cupcakes

A small batch of 9 cupcakes, just right for a little tea party.

Supplies

12 hole muffin tin, 9 paper liners, bowls, measuring jug and spoons, sieve, baking spatula or wooden spoon, whisk, teaspoon

Ingredients

250 mL (1 cup) plain flour

1$\frac{1}{2}$ tsp baking powder

pinch of salt

175 mL ($\frac{3}{4}$ cup) golden granulated sugar

5 Tbsp (75 g) unsalted butter, soft

1 large egg

175 mL milk

$\frac{1}{2}$ tsp vanilla extract

1 Preheat oven to 350°F (180°C).

2 Line the muffin tin with 9 paper liners.

3 Sift the flour, baking powder and salt into a bowl and mix.

4 In another bowl, use a baking spatula or wooden spoon to cream the sugar and butter. Switch to a whisk to stir in the egg. Gradually add the milk and vanilla. Stir in spoonfuls of the flour mixture until it is all added and the batter is smooth.

5 Spoon into the liners to about $\frac{3}{4}$ full. Bake 27 to 28 minutes, until the tops are golden and spring back when gently pressed or a toothpick stuck into the middle comes out clean. Cool completely before spreading with Tea Party Icing, or, if you don't mind some leftover icing, use one of the cake icings on pages 91–92.

Makes 9 Tea Party Vanilla Cupcakes.

Tea Party Icing

This light, fluffy icing will generously cover 9 cupcakes.

Supplies

bowls, measuring jug and spoons, sieve, small bowl or 500-mL measuring jug, rotary egg-beater, baking spatula, whisk

Ingredients

325 mL (1$\frac{1}{3}$ cups) golden icing sugar

125 mL whipping cream

sprinkle of salt

drop of vanilla extract

drop of natural food colouring

Sift the icing sugar into a bowl. Set aside.

In a small bowl or 500-mL measuring jug, use a rotary egg-beater to beat the cream and salt until fluffy. Scrape into a bowl. Use a whisk to stir in spoonfuls of the icing sugar until smooth and light. Stir in the vanilla and food colouring. Add a spoonful more icing sugar to thicken or a few drops of cream to thin, if needed.

Double Batch of Tea Party Vanilla Cupcakes

If you plan on having more friends visit, this is a batch of 18 cupcakes to share.

500 mL (2 cups) plain flour

1 Tbsp baking powder

$\frac{1}{4}$ tsp salt

375 mL (1$\frac{1}{2}$ cups) golden granulated sugar

150 g unsalted butter, soft

2 large eggs

375 mL milk

1 tsp vanilla extract

Follow the steps for 9 Tea Party Vanilla Cupcakes, except line two 12 hole muffin tins with 18 paper liners, and use the Double Batch of Tea Party Icing recipe or one of the cake icings on pages 91–92.

Double Batch of Tea Party Icing

This will generously cover 18 cupcakes.

650 mL (2$\frac{2}{3}$ cups) golden icing sugar

250 mL whipping cream

sprinkle of salt

a few drops of vanilla extract

1 or 2 drops of food colouring

Follow the steps for Tea Party Icing for 9 cupcakes.

Four Corners Chocolate Cake

Tea Party Vanilla Cupcakes, Chocolate Cupcakes

Four Corners Chocolate Cake

If you've got a 20-cm square tin, make this yummy cake.
Or fill 14 paper-lined muffin tins with the batter to make Chocolate Cupcakes.
They bake for about 27 minutes, or when a toothpick comes out clean. Ice the
cake or cupcakes with the icings on pages 91–92 or on the next page.

Supplies

20 x 20-cm square cake tin, parchment paper, bowls,
measuring jug and spoons, sieve, baking spatula or
wooden spoon, whisk, dinner knife, plate

Ingredients

300 mL (1$\frac{1}{4}$ cups) plain flour

5 Tbsp unsweetened cocoa powder

1$\frac{1}{2}$ tsp bicarbonate of soda

$\frac{1}{8}$ tsp salt

265 mL (1 cup + 1 Tbsp) golden granulated sugar

115 g unsalted butter, soft

1 large egg

250 mL milk

1 tsp vanilla extract

1 tsp white vinegar

1   Preheat oven to 350°F (180°C).

2   Grease and line the tin with parchment paper.

3   Sift the flour, cocoa powder, bicarbonate of soda and salt into a bowl and mix.

4   In another bowl, use a baking spatula or wooden spoon to cream together the sugar and butter. Use a whisk to stir in the egg, milk and vanilla (but not the vinegar yet). Don't worry if it's a little lumpy.

5   Still stirring with the whisk, mix in a few spoonfuls of the flour mixture at a time. When the batter is smooth, stir in the vinegar.

6   Scrape the batter into the tin and spread evenly. Bake about 35 minutes, or until a skewer inserted into the middle comes out clean. Cool completely.

7   To unmold the cake, run a dinner knife twice along the edges not covered by parchment. Hold on to the edges of the parchment paper and carefully lift out the cake. Or you can leave the cake in the tin and cut out squares as you eat them. Ice the cake, if you wish.

Makes 1 Four Corners Chocolate Cake.

Chocolate Cream Icing

A creamy icing with a classic chocolate taste.

Supplies

bowls, measuring jug, sieve, heatproof baking spatula, spoon

Ingredients

625 mL (2$\frac{1}{2}$ cups) golden icing sugar

2 squares semi-sweet chocolate (30 g each)

4 Tbsp whipping cream

5 Tbsp whipping cream

sprinkle of salt

drop of vanilla extract

Sift the icing sugar into a bowl. Set aside.

In a small bowl, heat the squares of chocolate and the 4 Tbsp cream at 50% power in the microwave until the chocolate is melted (about 2 to 3 minutes), stirring halfway. Use a heatproof baking spatula to stir smooth. Mix in the 5 Tbsp cream, salt and vanilla until smooth. Scrape into a bigger bowl.

Gradually spoon in the icing sugar and stir smooth. Add more icing sugar to thicken or a few drops of cream to thin, if needed.

Cow Coat Cupcakes

These are a variation on Tea Party Vanilla Cupcakes, but these have "patches" of chocolate cake. Can you see how they got their name?

Supplies

12 hole muffin tin, 9 paper liners, bowls, measuring jug and spoons, sieve, baking spatula or wooden spoon, whisk, 2 teaspoons

Ingredients

250 mL (1 cup) plain flour

1½ tsp baking powder

pinch of salt

175 mL (¾ cup) golden granulated sugar

5 Tbsp (75 g) unsalted butter, soft

1 large egg

175 mL milk

½ tsp vanilla extract

2 Tbsp unsweetened cocoa powder

½ tsp white vinegar

1 Preheat oven to 350°F (180°C).

2 Line the muffin tin with 9 paper liners.

3 Sift the flour, baking powder and salt into a bowl and mix.

4 In another bowl, use a baking spatula or wooden spoon to cream the sugar and butter. Switch to a whisk to stir in the egg, milk and vanilla. Add spoonfuls of the flour mixture as you stir until it has all been added and the batter is smooth.

5 Pour 250 mL of the batter into a large measuring jug or bowl. Use the whisk to stir in the cocoa powder completely, then stir in the vinegar.

6 Using a clean teaspoon for each batter, spoon overlapping blobs and layers into the paper liners. Do not stir the batter in the liners. Fill about ¾ full.

7 Bake 27 to 28 minutes, or until the tops spring back when gently pressed and a toothpick stuck in the middle comes out clean. Cool completely before icing with Tea Party Icing (page 98) or, if you don't mind some leftover icing, use one of the cake icings on pages 91–92.

Makes 9 Cow Coat Cupcakes.

Cow Coat Cupcakes

Tangy Lemon Loaf

Tastes a little like cake and bread all at once. You'll need 2 lemons to have enough juice for the loaf and the glaze.

Supplies

20 x 10-cm loaf tin, parchment paper, bowls, measuring jug and spoons, sieve, baking spatula or wooden spoon, juicer, whisk, baking rack, plate, spoon

Lemon Loaf

300 mL (1$\frac{1}{4}$ cups) plain flour

250 mL (1 cup) golden granulated sugar

1$\frac{1}{2}$ tsp baking powder

sprinkle of salt

115 g unsalted butter, cut into pieces

5 Tbsp fresh lemon juice

2 large eggs

$\frac{1}{2}$ tsp vanilla extract

Tangy Lemon Glaze

125 mL ($\frac{1}{2}$ cup) golden icing sugar

1 Tbsp fresh lemon juice

1 Preheat oven to 350°F (180°C).

2 Grease and line the loaf tin with parchment paper.

3 Sift the flour, sugar, baking powder and salt into a bowl and mix.

4 In another bowl, melt the butter in the microwave at 50% power (about 2 minutes). Cool.

5 Get help cutting the lemons in half. Squeeze the juice and spoon out the seeds. Measure 5 Tbsp juice and use a whisk to stir it into the melted butter. Mix in the eggs and vanilla.

6 Pour the butter mixture into the bowl of dry ingredients. Stir again with the whisk.

7 Scrape into the loaf tin with a baking spatula. Bake 40 to 45 minutes, or until golden and a skewer inserted into the middle comes out clean. Cool completely, then lift the lemon loaf out of the tin. Peel off the parchment. Put the loaf on a baking rack set on a plate (to catch glaze drips).

8 To make the glaze, sift the icing sugar into a bowl. Measure 1 Tbsp lemon juice and use a whisk to stir it into the icing sugar until smooth. Spoon over the loaf, letting it drip over the sides.
Let the glaze harden before slicing the loaf.

Makes 1 Tangy Lemon Loaf.

Tangy Lemon Loaf

Vanilla Cloud Cake

Vanilla Cloud Cake

An airy cake with a craggy top, like angel food cake. Delicious filled with lemon curd and dusted with icing sugar. Or top it with whipped cream and berries.

Supplies

15-cm round white ceramic souffle dish (not recommended for 20-cm round tins), parchment or wax paper, bowls, measuring jug and spoons, sieve, small bowl or 500-mL measuring jug, rotary egg-beater, baking spatula, whisk, dinner knife, plate

Ingredients

5 Tbsp plain flour

3 Tbsp cornflour

1 tsp baking powder

pinch of salt

2 large eggs

125 mL ($^1/_2$ cup) golden granulated sugar

$^1/_2$ tsp vanilla extract

125 mL lemon curd (shop-bought)

$^1/_2$ tsp golden icing sugar for dusting

1 Preheat oven to 350°F (180°C).

2 Grease and flour the sides of the souffle dish. Line the bottom with a round of parchment or wax paper.

3 Sift the flour, cornflour, baking powder and salt into a bowl and mix.

4 Put the eggs, sugar and vanilla into a small bowl or 500-mL measuring jug. Beat with a rotary egg-beater until thick, creamy and pale yellow. Use a baking spatula to scrape into a big bowl.

5 Use a whisk to gradually stir the flour mixture into the fluffy egg mixture. (Don't use the egg-beater to do this or the batter will be overbeaten.) Scrape into the souffle dish.

6 Bake about 35 minutes, or until the top is golden and a skewer inserted into the middle comes out clean. Cool completely.

7 To unmold the cake, run a dinner knife twice around the edge. Get help to tip the cake out. Peel the paper off the bottom. Get help slicing the cake in half cross-wise. Put the bottom half of the cake on a plate. Use a dinner knife to spread the lemon curd on the bottom cake. Replace the top of the cake and lightly dust with icing sugar.

Makes 1 Vanilla Cloud Cake.

Chocolate Mess Cakes

Messy and yummy. These are moist brown-sugar cakes with pockets of squishy chocolate and marshmallow.

Supplies

bowls, measuring jug and spoons, whisk, wooden spoon, four 9-cm round white ramekins or similar-sized baking cups, cup, baking sheet

Cakes

4 large marshmallows

4 Tbsp (60 g) unsalted butter, cut into pieces

5 Tbsp light muscovado brown sugar

4 Tbsp golden granulated sugar

1 large egg

1/2 tsp vanilla extract

5 Tbsp plain flour

5 Tbsp wholewheat flour

1/2 tsp baking powder

pinch of salt

Chocolate Mess

4 Tbsp water

2 Tbsp light muscovado brown sugar

1 Tbsp unsweetened cocoa powder

1 Pop the marshmallows into the freezer.

2 Preheat oven to 350°F (180°C).

3 To make the cake, melt the butter in a bowl at 50% power in the microwave (about 1 minute). Use a whisk to stir in the sugars. Cool slightly. Stir in rest of the ingredients for the cakes (but not the Mess) until smooth. Spoon into the 4 ramekins or baking cups, filling 2/3 full. Put a cold marshmallow in the middle of each cake.

4 To make the Chocolate Mess, put the ingredients in a cup and heat at 50% power in the microwave for 1 minute, until hot. Stir smooth. Pour over the marshmallows and cake batter.

5 Put the ramekins or baking cups on a baking sheet. Bake 23 minutes, or until puffed, the chocolate is bubbling and the marshmallows melt into top crusts. Cool until warm. Don't unmold. Scoop to eat.

Makes 4 Chcolate Mess Cakes.

Chocolate Mess Cakes   Lemon Pudding Cakes

Lemon Pudding Cakes

Bake two treats from 1 batter. Dig under the layer of airy
sponge cake to find a tart lemon pudding underneath.

Supplies

four 9-cm round white ramekins or similar-sized
baking cups, cups, measuring jug and spoons, juicer,
bowl, whisk, small bowl or 500-mL measuring jug,
rotary egg-beater, baking spatula, baking dish or
roasting tin large enough to hold the ramekins

Ingredients

2 Tbsp (30 g) unsalted butter

2 large egg yolks

4 Tbsp golden granulated sugar

2 Tbsp plain flour

125 mL milk

3 Tbsp fresh lemon juice (from one lemon)

2 large egg whites

pinch of salt

1 Preheat oven to 325°F (160°C).

2 Grease the 4 ramekins or baking cups.

3 Melt the butter in a cup in the microwave at 50%
power (about 30 seconds). Cool. Meanwhile, get
the lemon juice ready. Get help cutting a lemon in
half. Squeeze out the juice and remove the seeds.
Measure 2 Tbsp into a cup.

4 In a bowl, use a whisk to mix the cooled melted
butter, egg yolks and sugar. Stir in the flour, milk
and lemon juice until smooth.

5 Put the egg whites and salt in a small bowl or
500-mL measuring jug and beat with a rotary egg-
beater until fluffy. Use a baking spatula to scrape
the egg whites into the butter mix. Fold together.

6 Spread the batter in the ramekins or cups. Put them
inside the baking dish or roasting tin. Pour very
warm tap water into the tin (but don't splash any
into the ramekins or cups) until the water reaches
halfway up the sides.

7 Bake the ramekins or cups in the tin about 45 minutes, or until the top layer of cake turns spongy and
pale yellow. Remove from the oven and cool in the
pan until the ramekins are just warm to the touch
(about 15 minutes). Don't unmold. Scoop to eat.

Makes 4 Lemon Pudding Cakes.

NO !!

Peach-Topped Cake

A fruit-studded cake that's supposed to look a little messy on top. Don't bother to unmold it. Just cut and lift pieces out of the tin to eat.

Supplies

20-cm round metal cake tin, parchment or wax paper, bowls, measuring jug and spoons, sieve, whisk, baking spatula, cup

Ingredients

398 mL tinned peach slices or
    apricot halves

300 mL (1^1/$_4$ cups) plain flour

1 tsp baking powder

pinch of salt

1 large egg

150 mL (^{2}/$_3$ cup) golden granulated sugar

5 Tbsp milk

4 Tbsp vegetable oil

^{1}/$_2$ tsp vanilla extract

1 Tbsp granulated sugar, if you wish

5 Tbsp peach, apricot or orange jam

1 Preheat oven to 350°F (180°C).

2 Grease and flour the sides of the tin. Line the bottom with a round of parchment or wax paper.

3 Get help opening and draining the tin of fruit. Set aside.

4 Sift the flour, baking powder and salt into a bowl and mix.

5 In another bowl, use a whisk to mix the egg, sugar, milk, oil and vanilla. Pour into the flour mixture. Mix well with the whisk to make a batter. Use a baking spatula to spread the batter in the tin.

6 Place the pieces of drained fruit on the batter. Sprinkle the granulated sugar, if using, over top of the fruit.

7 Bake 55 to 60 minutes, or until the cake is golden and a skewer inserted into the middle comes out clean. Cool.

8 Put the jam in a cup and microwave at 50% power for about 30 seconds. Stir and spoon over the cake. Cool again before eating.

Makes 1 Peach-Topped Cake.

Peach-Topped Cake

Apple Sauce Cake

To make this moist cinnamon-scented cake, pay special attention to Step 5. You don't add all the egg and water. Bake the batter in either a 15-cm round souffle dish for a small, high cake or in a 20-cm round cake tin for a slightly bigger but flatter cake.

Supplies

15-cm round white ceramic souffle dish or 20-cm round cake tin, parchment or wax paper, bowls, measuring jug and spoons, sieve, baking spatula or wooden spoon, fork, whisk, dinner knife, plate

Ingredients

250 mL (1 cup) plain flour

1 tsp bicarbonate of soda

1/2 tsp cinnamon

pinch of salt

5 Tbsp light muscovado brown sugar

4 Tbsp golden granulated sugar

3 Tbsp (45 g) unsalted butter, soft

125 mL unsweetened apple sauce

1 large egg, plus cold water (see Step 5)

1 tsp white vinegar

1/2 tsp vanilla extract

1 Preheat oven to 350°F (180°C).

2 Grease and flour the sides of the cake tin. Line the bottom with a round of parchment or wax paper.

3 Sift the flour, bicarbonate of soda, cinnamon and salt into a bowl and mix.

4 In another bowl, use a baking spatula or wooden spoon to cream the brown and caster sugars and butter. Mix in the apple sauce. Set aside.

5 Crack the egg into a measuring jug and add enough cold water to reach the 125 mL level. Beat the egg and water with a fork or whisk. Add only 4 Tbsp of this to the apple sauce mixture. Stir well with the whisk. (Use the leftover egg mixture in scrambled eggs.)

6 Pour the apple sauce mixture into the flour mixture. Stir well with a whisk, then mix in the vinegar and vanilla. Scrape the batter into the dish or tin.

7 Bake 40 to 45 minutes, or until browned and a skewer inserted into the middle comes out clean. Cool until barely warm before unmolding. To unmold the cake, run a dinner knife twice around the cake. Get help tipping the cake out. Set right-side-up on a plate if eating plain. Set on a baking rack if glazing with Brown Sugar Glaze.

Makes 1 Apple Sauce Cake.

Brown Sugar Glaze

150 mL (²/₃ cup) golden icing sugar

2 Tbsp water

1 Tbsp light muscovado brown sugar

1 tsp unsalted butter

Sift the icing sugar into a bowl.

Mix the water and brown sugar in a small bowl and heat at 50% power in the microwave until the sugar dissolves (about 2 minutes). Use a spoon to stir in the butter until melted. Gradually spoon the sifted icing sugar into the melted sugar mix, stirring with a baking spatula until smooth. Spoon over Apple Sauce Cake, letting the glaze drip down the sides. Allow glaze to set before slicing.

Triple-Tier Fudge Cake

When you have a special occasion, make this spectacular cake from one tin. Plus, you can use the cake scraps and leftover icing for the easy Cake Truffles (page 119).

Supplies

22 x 32-cm metal baking tin, parchment paper, bowls, measuring jug and spoons, sieve, baking spatula or wooden spoon, whisk, paper, pencil, scissors, 3 toothpicks, small palette knife or dinner knife, plate

Ingredients

550 mL (2¼ cups) plain flour

2 tsp bicarbonate of soda

¼ tsp salt

3 squares unsweetened chocolate (30 g each)

375 mL (1½ cups) golden granulated sugar

115 g unsalted butter, soft

4 Tbsp vegetable oil

2 large eggs

2 tsp vanilla extract

175 mL milk

1 tsp white vinegar

sugar sprinkles and small sweets for decorating, if you wish

1 Preheat oven to 350°F (180°C).

2 Grease the tin and line with parchment paper.

3 Sift the flour, bicarbonate of soda and salt into a bowl and mix.

4 Put the chocolate squares in another bowl and heat at 50% power in the microwave until melted (about 3 minutes), stirring halfway. Stir smooth. Set aside to cool.

5 In a large bowl, use a baking spatula or wooden spoon to cream the sugar and butter. Mix in the oil, eggs, vanilla and cooled chocolate.

6 Use a whisk to gradually stir the flour mixture and milk into the butter mixture. Stir until the batter is smooth. Finally, mix in the vinegar.

7 Use a baking spatula to scrape the batter into the lined tin. Spread evenly. Bake about 40 minutes, or until a toothpick stuck in the middle comes out clean. Cool completely, then remove from the tin before cutting and assembling (page 116). Ice with Triple-Tier Fudge or White Chocolate Icing (pages 116 and 118).

Makes 1 Triple-Tier Fudge Cake.

Triple-Tier Fudge Cake, Cake Truffles

Triple-Tier Fudge Icing

This icing turns fudgy on the cake and slices well.

Ingredients

4 squares semi-sweet chocolate (30 g each)

4 Tbsp whipping cream

125 mL whipping cream

625 mL (2$\frac{1}{2}$ cups) golden icing sugar

$\frac{1}{4}$ tsp vanilla extract

sprinkle of salt

a few drops of milk (to thin, if needed)

Put the squares of chocolate and the 4 Tbsp whipping cream in a bowl and heat at 50% power in the microwave until the chocolate is melted (about 3 to 4 minutes), stirring halfway. Stir smooth and mix in the 125 mL cream. Use a rotary egg-beater to beat until thickened. Gradually beat in the icing sugar, vanilla and salt until fluffy. When the icing gets too stiff to beat, mix in the rest of the icing sugar with a spoon or baking spatula. If it's too stiff to spread, add a few drops of milk.

Makes enough icing for 1 Triple-Tier Cake and 1 batch of Cake Truffles (page 119).

How to Build a Triple-Tier Cake

1 Remove cake from the tin. Draw 3 circles on clean sheets of paper: 18, 12 and 8 cm in diameter. These are for tracing the cakes. Cut out the paper circles and arrange them on the cake without overlapping. Remember where they go. Push a toothpick through the centre of each paper circle, then stick it onto the cake. Don't press the toothpick through the paper and cake at the same time or you'll crack the cake. Get help cutting out the rounds of cake. (A sharp, serrated knife works best.)

2 Gently pull away the parts of the cake that are not part of the rounds. (Set aside the cake scraps for the Cake Truffles recipe, page 119.) Use a small palette knife or dinner knife to gently peel and lift the cake rounds off the parchment paper. Put the 18-cm round on a plate.

3 Ice the cake by scooping lots of Triple-Tier icing onto a baking spatula or palette knife. It is easier to start with too much icing than too little so the cake crumbs won't rub up as you spread the icing. Ice the 18-cm cake. Don't worry if the icing isn't perfect. Put the 12-cm round on the bottom cake and ice. Top with the 8-cm cake and ice. If you want to smooth out the icing, dip your spatula or knife in cold water and smooth over the big bumps. Add sprinkles and sweets before the icing sets, if you wish.

Triple-Tier White Chocolate Cake

This party cake is actually made in 1 tin, not 3. Use the cake scraps and leftover icing for the easy Cake Truffles (page 119).

Supplies

22 x 32-cm metal cake tin, parchment paper, bowls, measuring jug and spoons, sieve, heatproof baking spatula or wooden spoon, whisk, small bowl or 500-mL measuring jug, rotary egg-beater, paper, pencil, scissors, 3 toothpicks, small palette knife or dinner knife, plate

Ingredients

3 squares white chocolate (30 g each)

125 mL water

500 mL (2 cups) plain flour

1 Tbsp baking powder

1/4 tsp salt

250 mL (1 cup) golden granulated sugar

150 g unsalted butter, soft

2 large egg yolks

1 tsp vanilla extract

250 mL milk

2 large egg whites

sugar sprinkles and small sweets for decorating, if you wish

1 Preheat oven to 350°F (180°C).

2 Grease the tin and line with parchment paper.

3 Put the white chocolate and water in a bowl and heat at 50% power in the microwave until the chocolate is melted (about 3 minutes), stirring halfway. Stir smooth. Set aside to cool.

4 Sift and mix the flour, baking powder and salt in another bowl.

5 In a large bowl, use a baking spatula or wooden spoon to cream the sugar and butter. Mix in the egg yolks and vanilla. Gradually stir in the cooled white chocolate mixture.

6 Use a whisk to stir in spoonfuls of the flour mixture and splashes of milk, in turns, into the bowl of butter mixture. Make sure all of the flour mixture and milk gets mixed in. Set this batter aside.

7 Put the egg whites in a small bowl or 500-mL measuring jug. Beat with a rotary egg-beater until fluffy and white. Scrape into the bowl of batter and fold in. Scrape into the lined tin, spreading evenly. Bake about 40 minutes, or until the cake is golden and lightly browned at the edges and a toothpick stuck into the middle comes out clean. Cool completely, then remove from the tin before cutting and assembling. Frost with Triple-Tier Icing.

Makes 1 Triple-Tier White Chocolate Cake.

Triple-Tier White Chocolate Icing

A delectable creamy-coloured icing that firms up after spreading.

Ingredients

4 squares white chocolate (30 g each)

4 Tbsp whipping cream

5 Tbsp whipping cream

625 mL (2$\frac{1}{2}$ cups) golden icing sugar

$\frac{1}{4}$ tsp vanilla extract

pinch of salt

1 or 2 drops of natural food colouring, if you wish

a few drops of milk (to thin, if needed)

Put the squares of chocolate and the 4 Tbsp cream in a bowl and heat at 50% power in the microwave until the chocolate is melted (about 3 minutes), stirring halfway. Use a spoon or heatproof baking spatula to stir smooth. Stir in the 5 Tbsp cream until smooth. Scrape into a large bowl. Use a rotary egg-beater to gradually beat in the icing sugar, vanilla, salt and food colouring, if using, until fluffy. When the icing gets too stiff to beat, mix in the rest of the icing sugar with a spoon or baking spatula. If it's too stiff to spread, add a few drops of milk.

Makes enough icing for 1 Triple-Tier Cake and 1 batch of Cake Truffles (page 119).

See page 116 for how to build and ice a Triple-Tier Cake.

Cake Truffles

A delightful way to use up cake scraps and icing left over from Triple-Tier Cake recipes. Lovely made with either fudge or white chocolate flavours.

Supplies

bowls, measuring jug and spoons, pastry blender, wooden spoon, small dish

Ingredients

375 ml (1½ cups) scraps from Triple-Tier Cake
   (pages 114 and 117)

4 Tbsp leftover Triple-Tier Icing
   (pages 116 and 118)

a few drops of milk

your choice of *one* of the following as a coating:
   4 Tbsp ground almonds *or*
   2 Tbsp demerara sugar

1 Put the cake scraps in a bowl and use a pastry blender to break up into small crumbs. Measure 375 mL cake crumbs into another bowl.

2 In a bowl, stir the icing with a few drops of milk until it is creamy. Mix in the cake crumbs to make a cakey "dough."

3 Roll into balls slightly larger than 2.5 cm. Place your choice of ground almonds or sugar in a small dish. Roll cake balls in the coating. Chill until firm.

Makes about 12 Cake Truffles.

Pies, Pastries and Squares

Caramel Cookie Squares

Part cookie, part sweetie — the rich pastry is covered in a soft oven-baked caramel. This recipe is offered in 2 sizes. Choose 1 set of ingredients, but follow the same method for both.

Supplies

20 x 10-cm loaf tin or 20 x 20-cm square cake tin, parchment paper, bowls, measuring jug and spoons, baking spatula or wooden spoon, sieve, small bowl, baking rack

Loaf Tin

Cookie Layer

4 Tbsp (60 g) unsalted butter, soft

4 Tbsp golden granulated sugar

1 large egg yolk

150 mL (²⁄₃ cup) plain flour

pinch of salt

flour for dusting

Caramel Layer

125 mL (¹⁄₂ cup) light muscovado brown sugar

4 Tbsp plain flour

pinch of salt

4 Tbsp whipping cream

2 drops of vanilla extract

3 Tbsp chopped nuts, if you wish

OR

Square Tin

Cookie Layer

115 g unsalted butter, soft

125 mL (¹⁄₂ cup) golden granulated sugar

2 large egg yolks

325 mL (1¹⁄₃ cups) plain flour

pinch of salt

flour for dusting

Caramel Layer

250 mL (1 cup) light muscovado brown sugar

125 mL (¹⁄₂ cup) plain flour

pinch of salt

125 mL whipping cream

a few drops of vanilla extract

5 Tbsp chopped nuts, if you wish

1 Grease and line the tin with 2 pieces of parchment paper, criss-crossing them. Grease between the papers too so they stick together.

2 To make the cookie layer, use a baking spatula or wooden spoon to cream the butter and sugar in a bowl, then mix in the egg yolk(s). Sift in the flour and salt. Blend into a smooth dough. Scrape into the lined tin. Flour your hands and press the dough evenly in the bottom. Chill the tin of dough while you preheat the oven and make the caramel layer.

3 Preheat oven to 350°F (180°C).

4 To make the caramel layer, mix the brown sugar, flour and salt in a large bowl. Mash any sugar lumps with the back of a spoon. Set aside.

5 In a small bowl, heat the cream in the microwave at 50% power until it is hot (30 seconds to 1 minute). Pour into the brown sugar mixture, add the vanilla and mix well. Set aside.

6 Bake the chilled dough 15 minutes **for the loaf tin** size and 20 minutes **for the square tin** size. Cool a few minutes to avoid burning your hands when doing the next step (leave oven on).

7 Spread the caramel mixture on the dough and put back in the oven. **For the loaf tin,** bake about 20 minutes, until the caramel bubbles furiously and the edges are browned. **For the square tin,** bake about 25 minutes.

8 Take the tin out of the oven (the caramel will still be bubbling), place on a baking rack and immediately sprinkle on chopped nuts, if you wish. The caramel is gooey and very hot. Do not touch it yet. Cool completely before slicing.

Makes 1 batch Caramel Cookie Squares.

Caramel Cookie Squares

Peanut Butter Chocolate Bars

No-Cook Bars

Peanut Butter Chocolate Bars

These are rich, moist treats for peanut butter lovers. Use the kind that's your favourite — creamy or crunchy. This recipe is offered in 2 sizes. Choose 1 set of ingredients, but follow the same method for both.

Supplies

20 x 10-cm loaf tin or 20 x 20-cm square cake tin, parchment paper, bowl, measuring jug and spoons, baking spatula or wooden spoon

Loaf Tin

5 Tbsp light muscovado brown sugar

5 Tbsp peanut butter (creamy or crunchy)

1 Tbsp unsalted butter, soft

1 large egg

1/4 tsp vanilla extract

125 mL (1/2 cup) plain flour

3 Tbsp chocolate chips

OR

Square Tin

150 mL (2/3 cup) light muscovado brown sugar

150 mL (2/3 cup) peanut butter (creamy or crunchy)

2 Tbsp unsalted butter, soft

2 large eggs

1/2 tsp vanilla extract

250 mL (1 cup) plain flour

5 Tbsp chocolate chips

1 Preheat oven to 350°F (180°C).

2 Grease and line the tin with parchment paper.

3 In a bowl, use a baking spatula or wooden spoon to cream the brown sugar, peanut butter and butter. Add the egg and vanilla and mix well. Add the flour and mix well. Stir in the chocolate chips. You will have a soft dough. Drop blobs into the bottom of the lined tin. Press the dough in an even layer to the edges of the tin.

4 **For the loaf tin,** bake 20 to 25 minutes, until puffed and browned. **For the square tin,** bake 30 to 35 minutes. Cool completely. (The bars flatten as they cool.) Lift out and slice into bars or squares.

Makes 1 batch Peanut Butter Chocolate Bars.

No-Cook Bars

The ingredient list for this scrumptious no-bake recipe might look long, but some ingredients are used twice. Not a recipe for those who are squeamish about raw eggs. The recipe is offered in 2 sizes. Choose 1 set of ingredients, but use the same method for both.

Supplies

20 x 10-cm loaf tin or 20 x 20-cm square cake tin, parchment paper, bowls, measuring jug and spoons, heatproof baking spatula, sieve, wooden spoon

Loaf Tin
Bottom Layer

250 mL (1 cup) chocolate biscuit crumbs
   (or digestive biscuit crumbs)

125 mL (1/2 cup) desiccated coconut

3 squares semi-sweet chocolate (30 g each)

2 Tbsp (30 g) unsalted butter

1 Tbsp milk or cream

1/2 tsp vanilla extract

1 large egg yolk

Vanilla and Chocolate Layers

250 mL (1 cup) golden icing sugar

2 Tbsp vanilla custard powder

2 Tbsp (30 g) unsalted butter, very soft

2 Tbsp milk or cream

1/4 tsp vanilla extract

2 squares semi-sweet chocolate (30 g each)

1 Tbsp unsalted butter

OR

Square Tin
Bottom Layer

500 mL (2 cups) chocolate biscuit crumbs
   (or digestive biscuit crumbs)

250 mL (1 cup) desiccated coconut

6 squares semi-sweet chocolate (30 g each)

4 Tbsp (60 g) unsalted butter

2 Tbsp milk or cream

1 tsp vanilla extract

2 large egg yolks

Vanilla and Chocolate Layers

500 mL (2 cups) golden icing sugar

4 Tbsp vanilla custard powder

4 Tbsp (60 g) unsalted butter, very soft

4 Tbsp milk or cream

1/2 tsp vanilla extract

4 squares semi-sweet chocolate (30 g each)

2 Tbsp (30 g) unsalted butter

1   Line the tin with parchment paper. (You don't need to grease it.)

2   To make the bottom layer, mix the biscuit crumbs and coconut in a bowl.

3   In another bowl, heat the chocolate squares at 50% power in the microwave until melted (about 3 minutes for 3 squares or 3$\frac{1}{2}$ minutes for 6 squares), stirring halfway. Use a heatproof baking spatula to stir in the butter until smooth, then stir in the milk or cream and vanilla. Stir in the egg yolk until smooth. Scrape into the biscuit crumb mix and blend. Scrape into the lined tin. Press down in an even layer. Be careful not to let the parchment paper slip while pressing.

4   To make the vanilla layer, sift the icing sugar into a bowl. Stir in the vanilla custard or pudding powder. Use a clean baking spatula or wooden spoon to mix in the butter, milk or cream and vanilla until smooth. Spread evenly over the biscuit layer. Chill 15 minutes to set.

5   To make the chocolate layer, heat the chocolate squares in a small bowl at 50% power in the microwave until melted (about 2$\frac{1}{2}$ minutes for 2 squares and 3$\frac{1}{2}$ minutes for 4 squares), stirring halfway. Stir in the butter until smooth. Spread on top of the vanilla layer. Chill again for 15 minutes to set. Get help lifting the bars out of the tin and slicing. Keep chilled.

Makes 1 batch No-Cook Bars.

Classic Brownies

A perfect brownie that makes all fans happy since the recipe is both fudgy and cakey.

Supplies

20 x 20-cm baking tin, parchment paper, bowls, measuring jug and spoons, heatproof baking spatula, whisk

Ingredients

3 squares unsweetened chocolate (30 g each)

115 g unsalted butter, cut into pieces

150 mL ($^2/_3$ cup) light muscovado brown sugar

125 mL ($^1/_2$ cup) golden granulated sugar

1 Tbsp unsweetened cocoa powder

2 large eggs

1 Tbsp vegetable oil

$^1/_2$ tsp vanilla extract

150 mL ($^2/_3$ cup) plain flour

1 Preheat oven to 350°F (180°C).

2 Grease and line the tin with parchment paper.

3 In a small bowl, heat the squares of chocolate and the butter at 50% power in the microwave until the chocolate is melted (about 3 minutes), stirring halfway. Use a heatproof baking spatula to stir smooth.

4 In a big bowl, use the end of a whisk to break up the brown sugar until there are no lumps. Add the caster sugar, cocoa powder, eggs, oil and vanilla. Mix well. Use a baking spatula to scrape in the melted chocolate mixture. Blend well.

5 Add the flour a few heaping spoonfuls at a time. Mix well and scrape into the tin. Bake 25 minutes. Do not overbake or the brownies will not be fudgy. Cool completely in the tin before slicing. Top with Classic Brownie Glaze, if you wish.

Makes 1 batch Classic Brownies.

Classic Brownie Glaze

Ingredients

3 Tbsp (45 g) unsalted butter, cut into pieces

2 Tbsp milk, plus a few drops more if needed

250 mL (1 cup) golden icing sugar

3 Tbsp unsweetened cocoa powder

sprinkle of salt

2 or 3 drops of vanilla extract

In a small bowl, heat the butter and milk at 50% power in the microwave until the butter is melted (about 1$^1/_2$ minutes). Mix well.

Sift the icing sugar, cocoa powder and salt into a bowl and mix.

Use a baking spatula to scrape the melted butter mixture into the icing sugar mixture. Add the vanilla. Blend well. Add a few drops of milk to thin, if needed. Spread on Classic Brownies. Let stand a few minutes to set before slicing.

Makes enough glaze for 1 batch of Classic Brownies.

Cocoa Crunch Bars

A delicious twist on classic marshmallow treats — a little chewier and with a cocoa flavour.

Supplies

20 x 10-cm loaf tin, plastic wrap, measuring jug and spoons, glass bowl, heatproof baking spatula

Ingredients

750 mL (3 cups) white mini-marshmallows

3 Tbsp (45 g) unsalted butter, cut into pieces

1 Tbsp unsweetened cocoa powder

$^1/_4$ tsp vanilla extract

125 mL ($^1/_2$ cup) digestive biscuit crumbs

375 mL (1$^1/_2$ cups) puffed rice cereal

1 Line the loaf tin with plastic wrap. Pre-measure all your ingredients.

2 Place the marshmallows, butter and cocoa in the glass measuring cup or bowl. Heat at 50% power in the microwave to melt the marshmallows (about 1$^1/_2$ minutes). Stir with the heatproof baking spatula, return to microwave and heat again at 50% power for another 1$^1/_2$ minutes. The marshmallows will puff as they heat. They should be completely melted.

3 Place the cup of melted marshmallows on your work table and, working as quickly as you can with the heatproof baking spatula, stir in the vanilla, biscuit crumbs and puffed rice.

4 The mixture will begin to stiffen as you stir. While it is still soft, scrape it into the loaf tin and use the spatula to press it into an even layer. Chill about 20 minutes or until stiff. Holding the edges of the plastic wrap, lift out the Cocoa Crunch to slice.

Makes 1 batch Cocoa Crunch Bars.

Jam Cupboard Squares

When you don't have any fancy ingredients, you can still make these simple treats from ordinary stuff in the kitchen. This recipe is offered in 2 sizes. Choose 1 set of ingredients, but follow the same method for both.

Supplies

20 x 10-cm loaf tin or 20 x 20-cm square cake tin, parchment paper, bowl, measuring jug and spoons, baking spatula, spoon

Loaf Tin

5 Tbsp (75 g) unsalted butter, soft

4 Tbsp golden granulated sugar

1 large egg yolk

1 tsp milk

$1/4$ tsp vanilla extract

175 mL ($3/4$ cup) plain flour

sprinkle of salt

flour for dusting

4 Tbsp of your favourite jam

OR

Square Tin

150 g unsalted butter, soft

125 mL ($1/2$ cup) golden granulated sugar

2 large egg yolks

1 Tbsp milk

$1/2$ tsp vanilla extract

375 mL ($1 1/2$ cups) plain flour

sprinkle of salt

flour for dusting

125 mL ($1/2$ cup) of your favourite jam

1. Preheat oven to 350°F (180°C).

2. Grease and line the tin with parchment paper.

3. In a bowl, use a baking spatula to cream the butter and sugar. Mix in the egg yolk(s), milk and vanilla. Mix in the flour. Scrape the batter into the tin. Dust your fingers with flour and pat the sticky dough evenly over the pan bottom.

4. Bake the chilled dough 15 minutes **for the loaf tin** size and 20 minutes **for the square tin** size. Let cool slightly (keep oven on).

5. Stir the jam to loosen it and use the back of a spoon to spread the jam evenly over the pastry. **For the loaf tin,** bake another 20 minutes, until the edges are golden. **For the square tin,** bake another 25 minutes. Cool completely in the tin before slicing.

Makes 1 batch Jam Cupboard Squares.

Jam Cupboard Squares

Cocoa Crunch Bars

Lemon Squares

Cream Puffs

Lemon Squares

These have a thin layer of lemon curd on top. For the tangiest taste use fresh-squeezed juice.

Supplies

20 x 20-cm tin, parchment paper, bowls, measuring jug and spoons, baking spatula or wooden spoon, juicer, whisk

Pastry

115 g unsalted butter, soft

4 Tbsp golden granulated sugar

pinch of salt

250 mL (1 cup) plain flour

flour for dusting

Lemon Curd

175 mL ($^3/_4$ cup) golden granulated sugar

3 Tbsp plain flour

2 large eggs

4 Tbsp fresh lemon juice (from 1 large or 2 small lemons)

about 2 tsp golden icing sugar for dusting

1   Preheat oven to 350°F (180°C).

2   Grease and line the tin with parchment paper.

3   In a bowl, use a baking spatula or wooden spoon to cream the butter and sugar. Mix in the salt and flour to make a soft dough. Flour your hands and drop blobs of the dough into the lined tin. Press in an even layer to the edges of the pan. Bake 20 minutes.

4   To make the curd, get help cutting the lemon(s) in half. Squeeze the juice on a juicer. Remove any seeds. Measure out 4 Tbsp juice.

5   In a bowl, stir with a whisk sugar, flour, eggs and lemon juice until smooth.

6   When the dough has baked 20 minutes, remove the tin from the oven. Leave the oven on. Stir the lemon mixture and pour it on the baked dough. Get help putting the tin back into the oven and bake about 25 minutes. Get help to jiggle the tin to see if the lemon layer has set. The lemon should not wobble. Cool completely before dusting with icing sugar and slicing into squares.

Makes 1 batch Lemon Squares.

Cream Puffs

These fancy-looking pastries have never been easier to make. The fillings are shop-bought. Finish by dusting the puffs with icing sugar or spooning Chocolate Cream Puff Drizzle over top.

Supplies

baking sheet, parchment paper, measuring jug and spoons, large glass bowl, heatproof baking spatula or wooden spoon, tablespoon, dinner knife, small sieve for dusting icing sugar, if using

Ingredients

125 mL water

2 Tbsp (30 g) unsalted butter, cut into pieces

125 mL (1/2 cup) plain flour

1/8 tsp salt

1 large egg

250 mL whipped cream, or ice cream

2 tsp golden icing sugar for dusting, if you wish

1 Preheat oven to 400°F (200°C).

2 Line the baking sheet with parchment paper. Pre-measure the water, butter, flour and salt, and have the egg handy.

3 Put the water and butter into the glass bowl. Heat at 50% power in the microwave until the butter is melted and the water is hot (about 1 to 2 minutes).

4 Add the flour and salt to the hot water and butter. Using a heatproof baking spatula or wooden spoon, stir once or twice just to moisten before mixing in the egg. It will be slippery batter at first. Mix until there are no lumps of dry flour, but be sure the batter is slightly lumpy, like oatmeal.

5 Rub a little butter inside a tablespoon. Scoop slightly rounded tablespoons of the dough and drop in high mounds on the lined baking sheet. The lumpiness of the dough helps to make the mounds high. The higher your mounds, the rounder your cream puffs will be. Make 8 mounds, about 5 cm apart.

6   Bake about 25 minutes, until the cream puffs are risen and golden. Cool. Use a dinner knife to carefully cut each one in half cross-wise.

7   Spoon the filling of your choice onto the bottom half of each cream puff. Put the tops back on. Sift the icing sugar over top or spoon over Chocolate Cream Puff Drizzle.

Makes 8 Cream Puffs.

Chocolate Cream Puff Drizzle

125 mL ($\frac{1}{2}$ cup) golden icing sugar

1 Tbsp unsweetened cocoa powder

sprinkle of salt

1 Tbsp water, plus a few drops more to thin if needed

$1\frac{1}{2}$ tsp unsalted butter

1 or 2 drops of vanilla extract

Sift and mix the icing sugar, cocoa powder and salt in a bowl.

Heat the water and butter at 50% power in the microwave until the butter is melted (about 15 seconds). Stir in the vanilla. Pour this into the bowl with the icing sugar. Mix well. Add a few drops more water to thin, if needed. Spoon over filled Cream Puffs, letting the drizzle run down the sides.

Rocky Road Brownie Cups

These fancy brownies are baked in paper cups. The marshmallows turn slightly golden and delightfully chewy after baking.

Supplies

12 hole muffin tin, 8 paper liners, cup, bowls, measuring jug and spoons, heatproof baking spatula, fork, teaspoon

Ingredients

125 mL ($\frac{1}{2}$ cup) semi-sweet chocolate chips

4 Tbsp (60 g) unsalted butter, cut into pieces

$\frac{1}{2}$ tsp vanilla extract

125 mL ($\frac{1}{2}$ cup) plain flour

125 mL ($\frac{1}{2}$ cup) golden granulated sugar

pinch of salt

1 large egg

24 mini-marshmallows

4 Tbsp semi-sweet chocolate chips

2 Tbsp sliced almonds, if you wish

1 Preheat oven to 350°F (180°C).

2 Put the paper liners in the muffin tin.

3 In a cup or small bowl, microwave the chocolate chips and the butter at 50% power until melted (about 2 minutes). Stir in the vanilla with a heatproof baking spatula and set aside.

4 In another bowl, use a fork to mix the flour, sugar and salt. Use the baking spatula to scrape in the melted chocolate mixture and stir to moisten. Add the egg and mix well.

5 Using a teaspoon, drop the mix into the lined muffin tin. Fill each hole about $\frac{1}{3}$ full. Bake 15 minutes. Take the pan out of the oven and let it cool until the pan is no longer hot. Leave the oven on.

6 Place about 3 marshmallows and a few chocolate chips and almond slices, if using, on top of each brownie cup. Put back into the oven and bake another 6 or 7 minutes, until the marshmallows puff and begin to melt. Cool before eating.

Makes 8 Rocky Road Brownie Cups.

Rocky Road Brownie Cups

Sweet Snowflakes

Sweet Snowflakes

If your child can cut paper snowflakes, he or she can make these lacy pastries. They stay crunchy for days, so they can hang as decorations before being eaten.

Supplies

baking tray, parchment paper, small bowls or cups, measuring spoons, fork, teaspoon, damp cloth or paper towel, scissors, pastry brush, dinner knife

Ingredients

1 large egg white

2 Tbsp golden icing sugar

1 Tbsp golden granulated sugar

sprinkle of salt

2 Tbsp (30 g) unsalted butter

12 wonton wrappers (You won't need a whole packet. Wrap tightly and freeze the rest.)

1 Tbsp ground almonds, if you wish

1 Preheat oven to 350°F (180°C).

2 Line the baking tray with parchment paper.

3 In a small bowl, use a fork to beat the egg white, icing sugar, granulated sugar and salt until smooth. If there are lumps, mash them with the back of a teaspoon.

4 In a small cup or bowl, melt the butter at 50% power in the microwave (about 1 minute).

5 Peel off a wonton wrapper. (Cover the rest with a lightly dampened cloth or paper towel or they will dry out.) Fold the wrapper in fours — either on the diagonal or squared. Cut out edges and holes in the folded wrapper as you would with paper snowflakes. Don't make the cut-outs too big.

6 Open the snowflake and lay it flat on your work table. Use a pastry brush to lightly brush the top with melted butter. Turn it over and butter the other side too. Generously dab this top with the egg white mixture. (Brush only one side with egg mix.) Sprinkle the egg side with a little ground almond, if using.

7 Carefully peel the snowflake off the work surface and pat it flat on the lined baking sheet. A dinner knife might help you peel off the snowflakes. Make sure the egg side is facing up. Do the same for another 11 wrappers.

8 Bake 8 to 9 minutes, but watch very carefully in the last 2 minutes so the snowflakes don't burn. They should be very golden, browned at the edges and crispy through to the middle.

9 Remove from the oven. Cool completely before touching.

Makes 12 Sweet Snowflakes.

Bigger Snowflakes
You might also find egg roll wrappers in your super-market that look the same as wonton wrappers but are larger and sometimes round instead of square. You can make these into snowflakes, too. If they are larger, bake them 1 or 2 minutes longer until they are crispy and golden through to the middle.

Baby Lemon Meringue Pies

Fresh lemon juice gives these cute pies their sweet-tart taste. Make this recipe as either 2 small pies or 6 tarts. The little pie pans and tart pans are available in kitchenware shops or with the disposable aluminum bakeware in supermarkets.

Supplies

bowls, measuring jug and spoons, sieve, baking spatula or wooden spoon, two 12-cm pie tins or six 6-cm diameter tart tins, fork, glass bowl, whisk, juicer, baking tray, small bowl, rotary egg-beater

Pie or Tart Shells

150 mL (2/3 cup) plain flour

2 Tbsp golden icing sugar

1/4 tsp bicarbonate of soda

pinch of salt

3 Tbsp (45 g) unsalted butter, soft

1 Tbsp + 1 tsp vegetable oil

1/2 tsp golden granulated sugar

Filling and Meringue

150 mL (2/3 cup) golden granulated sugar

3 Tbsp cornflour

2 Tbsp plain flour

150 mL cold water

2 Tbsp fresh lemon juice (from 1 lemon)

1 Tbsp unsalted butter

2 large egg yolks

2 large egg whites

5 Tbsp golden caster sugar

1　Preheat oven to 350°F (180°C).

2　To make the pie or tart shells, sift and mix the flour, icing sugar, bicarbonate of soda and salt in a bowl.

3　In another bowl, use a baking spatula or wooden spoon to cream the butter, oil and granulated sugar. Gradually stir in the flour mixture. When it gets too stiff to stir, use your hands to knead in the rest of the flour mixture, keeping the dough inside the bowl.

4　Divide the dough into 2 equal pieces for the 2 small pies or 6 equal pieces for the tarts. Press evenly into the pie tins or tart tins. Neaten the pastry on the rim. Prick the pastry bottoms with a fork several times.

5　Chill the pastry while doing the next steps.

6　To make the filling, in a glass bowl, use a whisk to stir smooth the sugar, cornflour, flour and water. Heat at 50% power in the microwave to thicken (about 4 minutes), stirring halfway. Stir smooth again.

7　Get help cutting a lemon in half. Squeeze out the juice and remove the seeds. Whisk lemon juice and the butter into the hot mixture.

8　Cool to barely warm. Stir in the egg yolks.

9 Spread the filling in the chilled shells. Put on a baking tray. Bake the pies about 30 minutes and the tarts about 20 minutes. The shells should be lightly golden and the filling set and bubbling a little at the edges. Remove from the oven (but leave the oven on).

10 To make the meringue, beat the egg whites in a small bowl with a rotary egg-beater until fluffy and white. Gradually beat in the sugar until the meringue is white, glossy and fluffy.

11 Use a baking spatula to spread the meringue on the pies or tarts. Don't worry about making it too neat, as long as you cover the filling. Set back on the baking sheet. Bake 10 to 12 minutes, until the meringue has golden flecks. Cool completely before eating.

Makes 2 Baby Lemon Meringue Pies or 6 tarts.

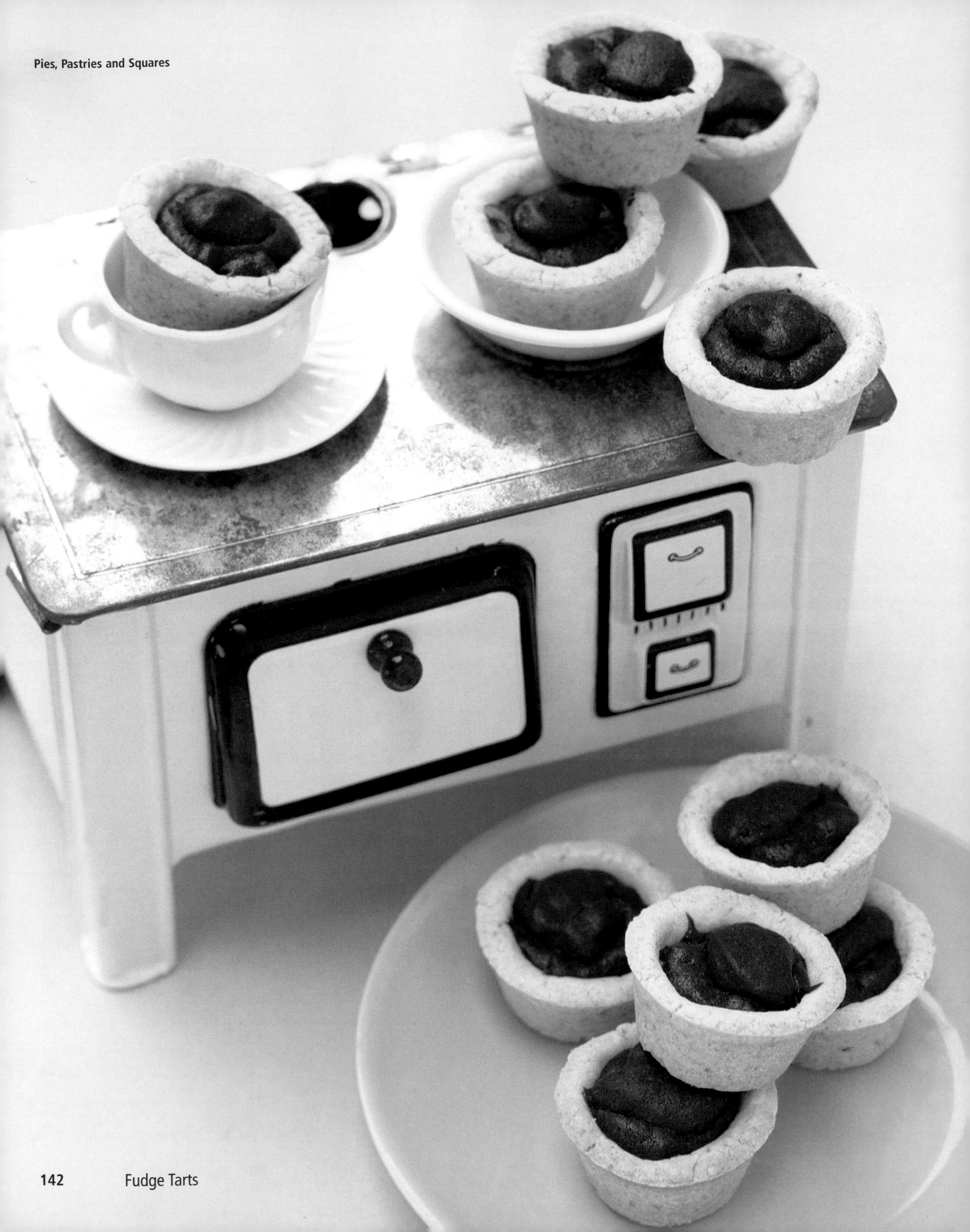

Fudge Tarts

Fudge Tarts

This recipe makes 11 delectable tarts — with some of the brownie-like filling left over to bake in paper cups as extra treats.

Supplies

bowls, measuring jug and spoons, baking spatula or wooden spoon, sieve, tablespoon, 24 hole mini-muffin tin, whisk, 5 mini-muffin paper liners

Tart Shells

3 Tbsp (45 g) unsalted butter, soft

1 Tbsp golden granulated sugar

1 large egg yolk

125 mL ($1/2$ cup) plain flour

4 Tbsp golden icing sugar

4 Tbsp bread crumbs

Filling

2 squares unsweetened chocolate (30 g each)

2 Tbsp (30 g) unsalted butter

5 Tbsp golden granulated sugar

1 large egg

$1^1/_2$ tsp plain flour

$1/4$ tsp vanilla extract

1 Preheat oven to 325°F (160°C).

2 To make the tart shells, use a baking spatula or wooden spoon to cream the butter and sugar until soft and mixed. Blend in the egg yolk.

3 Into another bowl, sift the flour and icing sugar. Add the bread crumbs and mix. Gradually mix into the butter mixture. When it gets too stiff to stir, knead in the rest of the flour mix to make a soft dough. If it sticks to your hands, knead in an extra sprinkling of flour.

4 Press pieces of the dough level inside a tablespoon. Put each spoonful of dough into the holes of a mini-muffin tin. Press the dough to line the bottom and sides of the tin. Make 11 tart shells. Chill the shells while you make the filling.

5 To make the filling, heat the chocolate squares and the butter at 50% power in the microwave until the chocolate is melted (about 2 to 3 minutes), stirring halfway. Cool slightly. Use a whisk to stir the sugar, egg, flour and vanilla until smooth. Spoon into the tart shells about half-full. Put mini-paper liners in 5 other holes of the mini-muffin tins and fill them half-full with leftover filling.

6 Bake 20 minutes, or until the filling is puffed and the edges of the tart shells are lightly browned. Cool completely.

Makes 11 Fudge Tarts and 5 fudge treats.

Little Butter Tarts

A buttery pastry holds a rich, brown-sugary soft filling.
The special tart dough doesn't toughen with handling.

Supplies

bowls, measuring jug and spoons, sieve, baking spatula or wooden spoon, tablespoon, 24 hole mini-muffin tin, whisk, paper towel, small spoon

Tart Shells

150 mL (²/3 cup) plain flour

2 Tbsp golden icing sugar

¹/4 tsp bicarbonate of soda

pinch of salt

3 Tbsp (45 g) unsalted butter, soft

1 Tbsp + 1 tsp vegetable oil

¹/2 tsp golden granulated sugar

Filling

2 Tbsp golden raisins, if you wish

2 Tbsp (30 g) unsalted butter, soft

2 Tbsp light muscovado brown sugar

1 large egg

pinch of salt

drop of vanilla extract

1   To make the tart shells, sift the flour, icing sugar, bicarbonate of soda and salt into a bowl and mix.

2   In a large bowl, use a baking spatula or wooden spoon to cream the butter, oil and sugar. Gradually stir in the flour mixture. When it gets too stiff to stir, use your hands to knead in the rest of the flour mixture, working inside the bowl.

3   Fill a tablespoon about half-full with dough. Press each piece onto the bottom and sides of a mini-muffin tin. Divide the dough among 11 holes of the muffin tin. The tart shells will be very thin; they puff a lot during baking. Chill at least 15 minutes while you make the filling.

4   Preheat oven to 375°F (190°C).

5   To make the filling, first decide if you want raisins. If you do, drop the raisins into a cup of hot water to plump up while you make the rest of the filling.

6   In a small bowl, use a baking spatula or wooden spoon to cream the butter and brown sugar. Use a whisk to mix in the rest of the ingredients, except the raisins, until smooth.

7   If you are adding raisins, drain them and pat dry with a paper towel. Drop a few into the bottoms of the chilled tart shells. Spoon filling into shells ³/4 full. Put into the oven and turn down the temperature right away to 325°F (160°C). Bake 20 to 22 minutes. The filling will puff up, but it settles back down when cooled. Cool tarts completely before removing from tin.

Makes 11 Little Butter Tarts.

Little Butter Tarts

Frozen Chocolate Cream Pie

The chocolate pastry tastes like a cookie and the creamy filling freezes firm but fluffy.
Not for those who are squeamish about raw egg whites.

Supplies

bowls, measuring jug and spoons, sieve, baking spatula or wooden spoon, 20-cm diameter pie tin, fork, baking sheet, 2 small bowls, rotary egg-beater

Pie Shell

175 mL (³/₄ cup) plain flour

4 Tbsp golden icing sugar

2 Tbsp unsweetened cocoa powder

pinch of salt

5 Tbsp (75 g) unsalted butter, soft

1 Tbsp golden granulated sugar

1 large egg yolk

1 tsp vegetable oil

Filling

4 squares sweetened chocolate (30 g each)

2 large egg whites

sprinkle of salt

250 mL whipping cream

¹/₂ tsp vanilla extract

2 tsp chocolate biscuit crumbs or grated chocolate for sprinkling, if you wish

1 To make the pie shell, sift the flour, icing sugar, cocoa powder and salt into a bowl and mix.

2 In another bowl, use a baking spatula or wooden spoon to cream the butter and sugar. Mix in the egg yolk and oil.

3 Gradually stir the flour mixture into the butter mixture. It will be a soft chocolate dough. Press evenly into the pie tin. Be sure the dough on the rim isn't too thin. Use a fork to prick the bottom of the pastry every inch or so. Chill 15 minutes.

4 Preheat oven to 350°F (180°C).

5 Put the pie shell on a baking sheet and bake 18 to 20 minutes, until the pastry isn't shiny anymore. Cool completely.

6 To make the filling, heat the squares of chocolate in a bowl at 50% power in the microwave for about 2 minutes. Stir, then heat for another 1 to 2 minutes, until melted. Stir again and cool to room temperature.

7 Put the egg whites and salt in a small bowl and beat with a rotary egg-beater until they are white and stiff.

8　In another small bowl, beat the cream and vanilla with the rotary egg-beater until thick and fluffy.

9　Use a baking spatula to gently fold the cooled chocolate into the whipped cream. Next, fold in the beaten egg whites. Spread the filling in the cooled pie shell. Sprinkle crumbs or grated chocolate on top, if you wish. Freeze about 2 hours, until firm. If the pie is too firm to cut, let it soften in the fridge or at room temperature.

Makes 1 Frozen Chocolate Cream Pie.

Fancy Fruit Flan

This looks like a cake-shop dessert. But in this recipe, the flan is a layer of cake rather than the traditional pastry crust.

Supplies

20-cm diameter by 2-cm deep tin with a loose bottom, baking sheet, bowls, measuring jug and spoons, baking spatula or wooden spoon, sieve, whisk, plate

Bottom and Topping

125 mL ($^1\!/_2$ cup) golden granulated sugar

2 Tbsp (30 g) unsalted butter, soft

1 large egg

$^1\!/_2$ tsp vanilla extract

sprinkle of salt

4 Tbsp milk

125 mL ($^1\!/_2$ cup) plain flour

$^1\!/_2$ tsp baking powder

150 mL soft custard

about 250 mL (1 cup) assorted fruit: your choice of fresh berries, banana slices, grapes or canned apricot halves, peach slices, orange segments

Glaze

2 tsp golden granulated sugar

2 tsp cornflour

125 mL water

2 tsp lemon juice

1 Preheat oven to 350°F (180°C).

2 Grease and flour the tart tin. Place on a baking sheet.

3 In a bowl, use a baking spatula or wooden spoon to cream the sugar and butter. Mix in the egg, vanilla and salt. Gradually mix in the milk.

4 In another bowl, sift and mix the flour and baking powder.

5 Use a whisk to gradually stir the flour mixture into the butter mixture. Blend well. Pour into the tart tin. Put the baking sheet with the tin into the oven and bake 25 to 26 minutes, or until the cake is golden. Cool completely before pushing out the flan, leaving the bottom of the tin under the cake. Put the cake on a serving plate.

6 Spread the vanilla pudding or custard over the cake. Arrange your fruit on top. Glaze if you wish.

7 To make the glaze, mix the sugar and cornflour in a bowl. Use a whisk to stir in the water and lemon juice. Mash out any lumps with a spoon. Heat at 50% power in the microwave until thickened (about $1^1\!/_2$ minutes). Stir smooth, then heat again at 50% power for another $1^1\!/_2$ minutes. Stir smooth. Cool slightly before spooning over fruit. Chill before eating.

Makes 1 Fancy Fruit Flan.

Fancy Fruit Flan

6

Candies, Confections and Cool Treats

Apple Pie Ice Cream

Who'd guess that a cold treat with the flavour of a hot dessert would taste so good?

Supplies

bowls, measuring jug and spoons, heatproof baking spatula, small bowl, rotary egg-beater, 20 x 10-cm loaf tin (preferably the disposable aluminum kind since freezing may harm regular bakeware) or a freezer-safe bowl or about 6 small paper cups

Ingredients

2 squares white chocolate (30 g each)

125 mL whipping cream

1 large egg

125 mL ($1/2$ cup) golden granulated sugar

150 mL plain yogurt (1% milk-fat or higher)

125 mL unsweetened apple sauce

$1/8$ tsp cinnamon

3 or 4 drops of vanilla extract

2 Tbsp digestive biscuit crumbs

1   Put the white chocolate squares and the cream in a bowl and heat in the microwave at 50% power for 2 minutes. Using a heatproof baking spatula, stir, then heat another 2 minutes to melt the chocolate. Stir smooth and let stand while you do the next step.

2   Put the egg in a small bowl. Beat with the rotary egg-beater until thick and creamy. Gradually beat in the sugar.

3   Pour the egg mixture into the chocolate mixture. Beat to blend. Heat this mixture at 50% power in the microwave for 2 minutes. Stir, then heat again for another minute to thicken. Stir smooth. Cool slightly.

4   In another bowl, mix the yogurt, apple sauce, cinnamon and vanilla. Add the white chocolate mixture to this and mix well. Pour the biscuit crumbs on top and swirl them into the mix, but do not blend them in completely.

5   Pour into the loaf tin, freezer-safe bowl or paper cups. Freeze at least 3 hours, until set. Press gently in the middle to check if it has frozen through. If it is too hard to scoop, let stand at room temperature for a few minutes to soften.

Makes 1 batch Apple Pie Ice Cream.

Apple Pie Ice Cream

Chocolate Sprinkles Ice Cream

Chocolate Sprinkles Ice Cream

This rich ice cream already has sprinkles on it when you scoop. Use the recipe also for fudgy pops, if you have moulds — but don't add the sprinkles.

Supplies

bowls, measuring jug and spoons, whisk, rotary egg-beater, heatproof baking spatula, 20 x 10-cm loaf tin (preferably the disposable aluminum kind since freezing can harm regular bakeware) or a freezer-safe bowl or about 6 small paper cups or freezer pop moulds

Ingredients

1 large egg

125 mL (1/2 cup) golden granulated sugar

125 mL whipping cream

2 squares semi-sweet chocolate (30 g each)

125 mL plain yogurt (2% milk-fat or higher)

1/2 tsp vanilla extract

1 to 2 tsp sprinkles

1   In a small bowl, use a whisk to mix the egg and sugar. Beat with a rotary egg-beater until thick, creamy and pale yellow. Add the cream and beat until blended.

2   Heat at 50% power in the microwave for 2 minutes, or until slightly thickened at the edges. Stir with a heatproof baking spatula until smooth. Heat for another 2 minutes at 50% power. Stir smooth.

3   Put the chocolate squares in another bowl and heat at 50% power in the microwave until melted (about 2 to 3 minutes), stirring halfway. Using the heatproof spatula, stir the melted chocolate into the egg mixture. Blend well. Cool to room temperature.

4   Stir the yogurt and vanilla into the cooled chocolate mix. Beat with the rotary egg-beater until light and creamy. Pour into the loaf tin, bowl, paper cups or freezer pop molds. Scatter sprinkles on top of the loaf tin, bowl or cups. (Do not stir.)

5   Freeze about 3 hours, until firm. If it is too hard to scoop, let stand at room temperature for a few minutes to soften.

Makes 1 batch Chocolate Sprinkles Ice Cream.

Chocolate-Swirled Fruit

A quick dip in two kinds of melted chocolate gives a striped coating to strawberries, cherries or orange segments.

Supplies

baking sheet or tin, parchment or wax paper, small bowl, spoon

Ingredients

1 square semi-sweet chocolate (30 g)

1 square white chocolate (30 g)

about 8 strawberries, cherries, orange segments or other pieces of fruit

1   Line the baking sheet or tin with parchment or wax paper. Be sure the fruit is dry so the chocolate sticks properly.

2   In a small bowl, put the square of semi-sweet chocolate on the bottom and top with the white chocolate. The white chocolate must be stacked on top of the semi-sweet chocolate so the white chocolate doesn't touch the bowl and scorch during melting. Heat at 50% power in the microwave until melted (about 3 minutes), stirring once around the bowl halfway through. To make sure you get bold swirls, do not overmix.

3   Holding one end of a piece of fruit, dip it into the melted chocolate. Pull the fruit through the chocolate in one motion. To make sure you get swirls, don't wiggle the fruit in the chocolate. Set the dipped fruit on the lined baking sheet or tin. Chill about 15 minutes, until the chocolate hardens. Eat cold.

Makes about 8 pieces of Chocolate-Swirled Fruit.

Banana Malted Ice Cream, Frozen Strawberry Yogurt   Chocolate-Swirled Fruit, Needles in Haystacks

Needles in Haystacks

These nutty chocolate treats don't need baking, just the microwave
for melting and the fridge for chilling.

Supplies

baking sheet, parchment or wax paper, bowl, heat-proof baking spatula, measuring jug and spoons, spoon

Ingredients

4 squares semi-sweet chocolate (30 g each)

125 mL ($1/2$ cup) desiccated coconut

125 mL ($1/2$ cup) slivered almonds

2 Tbsp digestive biscuit crumbs

1 Line the baking sheet with parchment or wax paper. Pre-measure all the ingredients.

2 In a bowl, heat the chocolate at 50% power in the microwave for 2 to 3 minutes. Use a heatproof baking spatula to stir and heat again for another minute, until melted.

3 Add the remaining ingredients and stir to coat with the chocolate.

4 Using a spoon, scoop mounds of the mixture and push them onto the lined baking sheet. Chill about 20 minutes, until firm.

Makes about 15 Needles in Haystacks.

Banana Malted Ice Cream

Bananas are delicious with chocolate. Two ripe ones go into this recipe.

Supplies

heavy plastic bag, rolling pin or coffee mug, bowl, potato masher or fork, measuring cups and spoons, small bowl or 500-mL measuring jug, rotary egg-beater, baking spatula, about 6 small paper cups

Ingredients

75 mL chocolate-covered malted milk balls, like maltesers (40 g, about 17 balls)

2 ripe bananas

2 tsp lemon juice

175 mL whipping cream

3 Tbsp golden granulated sugar

1/4 tsp vanilla extract

1 Tbsp chocolate malted drink powder, if you wish

whole malted milk balls for garnish, if you wish

1. Put the malted milk balls in a heavy plastic bag and carefully smash with a rolling pin or the bottom of the coffee mug until they are roughly crushed. The pieces should be different sizes. Don't smash all the balls into a powder.

2. Peel the bananas and put them into a bowl. Mash them to a smooth pulp with a potato masher or fork. You should have about 250 mL of mashed banana. Stir in the lemon juice.

3. Put the cream into a small bowl or 500-mL measuring jug and beat with a rotary egg-beater until thickened. (It will look like melted ice cream.) Gradually beat in the sugar until thick and creamy. Do not overbeat to stiff peaks. Scrape the beaten cream and the vanilla into the bowl of mashed bananas and mix well. Use a baking spatula to gently fold in the crushed malted milk balls, vanilla and malt powder, if using.

4. Pour into the paper cups. Top with whole malted milk balls for garnish, if you wish. Freeze about 3 hours, until firm. Press gently in the middle to check if it has frozen through. If it is too hard to scoop, let stand at room temperature for a few minutes to soften.

Makes 1 batch Banana Malted Ice Cream.

Frozen Strawberry Yogurt

This is halfway between a frozen yogurt and an ice cream — bursting with the taste of fresh strawberries.

Supplies

paper towel, dinner knife, bowl, potato masher or fork, measuring jug, baking spatula, small bowl, rotary egg-beater, about 6 small paper cups

Ingredients

250 mL (1 cup) fresh strawberries

125 mL plain yogurt (1% milk-fat or higher)

125 mL whipping cream

4 Tbsp golden caster sugar

1 Wash the strawberries and pat dry with a paper towel. Cut off the stems with a dinner knife. Don't cut off too much of the berry, but be sure there are no hard stem parts left. Cut each strawberry in half. Put them in a bowl and mash into a pulp with a potato masher or fork.

2 Stir the yogurt into the mashed strawberries.

3 In a small bowl, beat the cream with a rotary egg-beater until thickened. (It will look like melted ice cream.) Gradually beat in the sugar. The mixture should be thick and creamy. Don't overbeat or else the cream will get a buttery taste.

4 Scrape the beaten cream into the strawberry mixture with a baking spatula. Blend well.

5 Pour into the paper cups. Freeze about 3 hours, until firm. Press gently in the middle to check if it has frozen through. If it is too hard to scoop, let stand at room temperature for a few minutes to soften.

Makes 1 batch Frozen Strawberry Yogurt.

Roasted Cinnamon Nuts

These bake up crunchy and fill the house with a wonderful aroma.

Supplies

baking sheet, parchment paper, bowl, measuring jug and spoons, whisk, spoon

Ingredients

1 large egg white

4 Tbsp golden icing sugar

1/2 tsp vanilla extract

1/4 tsp cinnamon

tiny pinch of nutmeg

2 drops of orange extract, if you wish

375 mL (1 1/2 cups) walnut or pecan halves

1 Preheat oven to 325°F (165°C).

2 Line the baking sheet with parchment paper.

3 In a large bowl, use a whisk to mix the egg white, icing sugar, vanilla, cinnamon, nutmeg and orange extract, if using, until smooth. Pour in the nuts and stir with a spoon to coat them with the syrup. Grab handfuls of nuts — let the extra syrup fall back into the bowl — and spread them on the lined baking sheet. Wash your hands.

4 Bake the nuts in the oven for about 20 minutes, until they look dried and golden and you can smell a delicious nutty aroma.

Makes 375 mL (1 1/2 cups) Roasted Cinnamon Nuts.

Roasted Cinnamon Nuts

Classic Chocolate Fudge, Maple Nut Fudge

Classic Chocolate Fudge

This yummy recipe isn't cooked on the cooker, which means no sticky pot to clean. The fudge starts as thick and pourable but quickly firms up as it cools.

Supplies

measuring jug and spoons, 15 x 8-cm mini-loaf tin or 10- or 12-cm round or square flat-bottomed dish or food storage container, plastic wrap, bowl, heatproof baking spatula

Ingredients

125 mL sweetened condensed milk

6 squares semi-sweet chocolate (30 g each)

1/2 tsp unsalted butter

1/4 tsp vanilla extract

4 Tbsp chopped walnuts or pecans, if you wish

1 Pre-measure all the ingredients and line the dish before you start. To line, rub the inside of the dish with vegetable oil. Line it with plastic wrap, pressing the wrap as smoothly as you can against the bottom, and up and over the sides.

2 Put the condensed milk and chocolate squares in a bowl. Heat at 50% power in the microwave 2 minutes. Use a heatproof baking spatula to stir, then heat for another minute to melt the chocolate. If it has not melted, heat another 30 seconds. Stir smooth.

3 Mix in the rest of the ingredients. Still using the spatula, fold over and press down the fudge a few times until it is smooth. Place in the lined dish and press the fudge flat with the blade of the spatula. Chill in the fridge about 10 minutes, until set. Lift the fudge out and get help cutting it into pieces.

Makes 1 batch Classic Chocolate Fudge.

Maple Nut Fudge

Just the right amount of fudge to satisfy your sweet tooth. The fudge starts as a thick and pourable but quickly firms up as it cools.

Supplies

measuring jug and spoons, 15 x 8-cm mini-loaf tin or 10- or 12-cm round or square flat-bottomed dish or food storage container, plastic wrap, bowl, heatproof baking spatula

Ingredients

2 Tbsp light muscovado brown sugar

4 Tbsp sweetened condensed milk

6 squares white chocolate (30 g each)

2 Tbsp maple syrup or runny honey or 1 Tbsp for a firmer fudge

1/4 tsp vanilla extract

sprinkle of salt

4 Tbsp whole pistachios, or chopped walnuts and pecans, if you wish

1 Pre-measure all the ingredients and line the dish before you start. To line, rub the inside of the tin or dish with vegetable oil. Line it with plastic wrap, pressing the wrap as smoothly as you can against the bottom, and up and over the sides.

2 Mix the brown sugar and condensed milk in a bowl. Place the white chocolate in the same bowl. Heat at 50% power in the microwave for 2 minutes, then use a heatproof baking spatula to stir. Heat for another minute to melt the chocolate. If it has not melted, heat another 30 seconds. Stir smooth.

3 Mix in the rest of the ingredients. Still using the spatula, fold over and press down the fudge a few times until it is smooth and the maple syrup is blended in, not runny. Place in the lined dish and press the fudge flat with the blade of the spatula. Chill in the fridge about 10 minutes, until set. Lift the fudge out and get help cutting it into pieces.

Makes 1 batch Maple Nut Fudge.

Sweet Marbles

These are very sweet and fun to make if you have a gang of kids coming over.
It's a no-cook recipe where each beautiful marble is unique.

Supplies

bowls, measuring jug and spoons, tablespoon, baking spatula or wooden spoon, sifter, 3 small plastic bags

Ingredients

4 Tbsp sweetened condensed milk

4 Tbsp corn syrup

1 Tbsp unsalted butter, soft

pinch of salt

750 mL (3 cups) golden icing sugar (plus a few spoonfuls, if necessary)

3 or 4 assorted natural food colourings

1   In a large bowl, use a baking spatula or wooden spoon to mix the condensed milk, corn syrup, butter and salt.

2   Sift the icing sugar into another bowl. Stir the icing sugar into the corn syrup mixture a couple of large tablespoons at a time. The candy will get stiffer as you add more icing sugar. Keeping the candy inside the bowl, knead it with your hands until there is no loose icing sugar left. You should have a firm, smooth candy the texture of play dough. If the candy is sticking to your hands, knead in a few more spoonfuls of icing sugar to firm it up.

3   Divide the candy into 4 roughly equal pieces. Put one piece in each of the plastic bags, leaving a piece in the bowl. Put a drop or two of food colouring into each plastic bag (keep each bag a different colour), seal the bags and use your hands to mash the colouring into the candy. Keep the candy in the bowl uncoloured.

4   To make the marbles, pinch off little pieces of the coloured and white candies, squeeze them together and roll into a ball. For a different effect, shape some of the candy into long strips before squeezing with the other colours and rolling into balls. Keep the balls chilled as you finish rolling.

Makes about 2 dozen Sweet Marbles.

Sweet Marbles   Strawberry-Fudge Layer Cake

Strawberry-Fudge Layer Cake

Turn digestive biscuits into soft cake sandwiched between layers of strawberry cream. All you need is the patience to wait overnight.

Supplies

small bowl, measuring jug and spoons, rotary egg-beater, cup, spoon, baking spatula, 20 x 10-cm or slightly larger loaf tin, bowl, sieve, whisk

Layered Cake

150 mL whipping cream

2 tsp golden granulated sugar

125 mL strawberry jam

1 packet digestive biscuits (you won't use it all)

Fudge Glaze

175 mL (3/4 cup) golden icing sugar

3 Tbsp unsweetened cocoa powder

2 Tbsp water

1 Tbsp unsalted butter

1/4 tsp vanilla extract

1   To make the cake, use a rotary egg-beater to beat the cream and sugar in a small bowl until fluffy. Put the jam in a small cup and stir with a spoon to loosen. Use a baking spatula to mix the jam into the whipped cream.

2   Cover the bottom of the loaf tin with a single layer of digestive biscuits. Make sure the biscuits reach the sides of the tin. Break off pieces of biscuit to fill in any gaps. Don't worry if it looks messy.

3   Spread 5 Tbsp of the strawberry cream over the layer of biscuits with the baking spatula. Put another layer of biscuits on top of the strawberry cream. Press down gently on the biscuits to push out big air bubbles. Keep making layers with the biscuits and strawberry cream. You will get 5 biscuit layers and 4 cream layers. Finish with a biscuit layer on top. Be sure to leave about a 1-cm space at the top of the tin.

4   To make the fudge glaze, sieve the icing sugar and cocoa powder into a bowl.

5   Put the water and butter in a cup and heat at 50% power in the microwave until the butter is melted (about 30 seconds). Use a whisk to stir the hot water mixture into the icing sugar mixture. Add the vanilla and stir until smooth. Pour over the loaf. Chill overnight. Slice or scoop to eat.

Makes 1 Strawberry-Fudge Layer Cake.

Toasted Coconut Milkmallows

These chilled marshmallows don't require cooking. They're light as a cloud, not too sweet and rolled in nutty toasted coconut. Not for those squeamish about raw egg whites.

Supplies

15-cm diameter flat-bottomed dish or food storage container, plastic wrap, cups, fork or small whisk, small bowl, rotary egg-beater, baking spatula, baking sheet, parchment paper, dinner knife or 4-cm round cutter

Ingredients

1 Tbsp unflavoured gelatin powder (1 packet)

2 Tbsp water

4 Tbsp water

2 Tbsp golden granulated sugar

2 Tbsp skimmed milk powder

2 large egg whites

sprinkle of salt

125 mL desiccated coconut

1. Rinse the inside of the dish or container with cold water. (The water helps the plastic wrap stick on tightly.) Line the dish or container with plastic wrap, pressing it as smoothly as you can against the bottom, and up and over the sides.

2. In a small cup, mix the gelatin with the 2 Tbsp water. Let it stand while you do the next steps.

3. In a cup, mix the 4 Tbsp water, sugar and milk powder. Heat at 50% power in the microwave 1 1/2 minutes. Add the lump of softened gelatin to the hot milk mixture and stir with a fork or small whisk until it dissolves. Set aside.

4. Put the egg whites and salt in a small bowl. Use a rotary egg-beater to beat the egg whites until they are fluffy and white. No liquid egg should be left in the bottom of the bowl. Pour in half of the milk mixture. Beat. Then pour in the rest of the milk mixture and beat again.

5. Use a baking spatula to scrape the fluffy mix into the plastic-lined dish. Spread out evenly into a 2.5-cm thick layer of milkmallow. Chill about 15 minutes.

6. Preheat oven to 350°F (180°C).

7. Line a baking sheet with parchment paper and spread the coconut on it. Toast in the oven for 2 to 3 minutes, until the shreds begin to turn golden. Watch carefully to avoid burning. Cool.

8. After chilling the milkmallow, gently pull on the plastic at the edges to lift the layer of milkmallow out of the dish. Dip the round cutter (if using) in cold water and cut 12 rounds. Or dip a dinner knife in cold water and slice the milkmallow into 24 cubes. Roll all sides of each milkmallow in the toasted coconut. Keep chilled.

Makes 12 round or 24 cubed Toasted Coconut Milkmallows.

Toasted Coconut Milkmallows   Dinosaur Eggs

Dinosaur Eggs

A laugh to make with friends. The thick meringue bakes into almost hollow "egg shells" containing a lining of marshmallow. Some of the eggs will crack while they bake, looking like they've hatched.

Supplies

baking sheet, parchment paper, measuring jug and spoons, small bowl, rotary egg-beater, teaspoon

Ingredients

1 large egg white

sprinkle of salt

125 mL (1/2 cup) golden granulated sugar

cold water

1/2 tsp chocolate malted drink powder or fruit-flavoured gelatin powder

1 Preheat oven to 350°F (180°C).

2 Line a baking sheet with parchment paper.

3 Place the egg white and the salt in a small bowl. Beat with the rotary egg-beater until fluffy. Gradually beat in the sugar until it is stiff and white. You might need help with this part. Once the mixture gets too thick to beat, stir in the rest of the sugar with a spoon. The mixture must be thick enough to form stiff mounds.

4 Use a teaspoon to scoop about a walnut-sized blob of the fluffy egg whites (this is called meringue) and push it off the spoon onto the baking sheet with your finger. The more oval and higher these meringue mounds are, the more they will look like eggs after they are baked. To shape the meringue, dip your finger in cold water and gently push the bottom edges of the mounds into ovals and smooth the tops of the mounds by gently patting down any peaks.

5 Make 10 mounds, about 8 cm apart. Wash and dry your hands.

6 Sprinkle each mound with a little bit of the malted milk powder or flavoured gelatin powder to add extra taste and make speckles on the eggs. Sprinkle the powder from a few inches above the meringues to spread it evenly. If you sprinkle too close to the mounds, you will get heavy blobs. Leave some of the eggs plain, if you wish.

7 Bake 12 minutes, or until the eggs puff and form a hard outer shell. Some will crack — they're supposed to. Cool completely on the sheet before removing.

Makes 10 Dinosaur Eggs.

Glossary

Baking powder: A powder that helps cakes and biscuits rise. Do not confuse with bicarbonate of soda.

Bicarbonate of soda: Also called baking soda or sodium bicarbonate.

Brown sugar: Billingtons range of unrefined sugars are the ones recommended in the recipes but you could use any brown or dark brown sugar. Be sure the sugar is soft so it can be firmly packed into the measuring jug or cup until level. The darker the sugar, the more molasses flavour the recipe will have.

Butter, soft: Let cold butter stand at room temperature for several hours or overnight to soften. See also Unsalted Butter.

Chill: To chill in the refrigerator.

Chocolate: Baking chocolate usually sold in bars with 30-g squares. Available in semi-sweet, sweetened, unsweetened, bittersweet and white chocolate varieties. When chocolate squares are melted in the microwave at 50% power, they retain their shape while turning "wet" and glossy looking. They will not melt into a puddle. To ensure melting, heat at the times specified in the recipes, stirring halfway. Check if the chocolate has melted by dipping into it with a spoon. If there is still unmelted chocolate, heat at 50% power for additional 30-second increments.

Chocolate chips: Use either milk or dark chocolate chips. These are sweetened.

Cool: To cool at room temperature. Do not confuse with chilling.

Corn syrup: Some of the recipes use corn syrup, you must not use golden syrup instead, they are not the same and it would affect the way the recipe turns out. If you cannot get corn syrup do not prepare the recipe. You can buy corn syrup direct from The Rosslyn Delicatessen, 56 Rosslyn Hill, London NW3 (tel: 020 7794 9210) and they will sell bottles by mail order.

Cream: To use a baking spatula or wooden spoon to mash together until they are completely mixed, usually for butter and sugar.

Eggs: Use large eggs for best results. For notes on separating eggs, please see "Basic Tools" in the "Organizing the Kitchen" chapter.

Fold: To use a baking spatula to gently mix beaten eggs with other ingredients. In this book, the eggs are usually scraped into a bowl of other ingredients. To fold, cut down to the bottom of the bowl with the spatula, slide it under the mixture, then bring the spatula back up. Repeat this motion to turn the mixture over until it is blended. It should stay as fluffy as possible.

Food colouring: Natural food colourings are strongly recommended because of the possible reactions or allergies some children experience to artifical colourings. Supercook, the brand most easily found in supermarkets, do a natural red and natural yellow, all their other colours are artificial. The Spice Shop in Blenheim Crescent, London W11 do a tasteless beetroot powder which gives a bright dark purple colour to food and also a tasteless spinach powder which provides a green colour. Their products can be purchased from the shop or via their web site www.thespiceshop.co.uk

Granulated sugar: Recipes use Billingtons golden granulated sugar because it is unrefined but you can use normal granulated sugar.

Grated cheese: Either purchase grated cheese or helpers can grate. Children are not expected to use graters.

Icing sugar: Recipes use Billingtons golden icing sugar since it is unrefined but you can use ordinary. Also called confectioners' sugar. Please see "Measuring Ingredients" in the "Organizing the Kitchen" chapter.

Measuring cups: If you decide to use measuring cups you must purchase a set of proper measuring cups, do not use just an ordinary tea cup. Lakeland Limited do sets of plastic ones.

Milk: Use cow's milk with 1% milk-fat or higher.

Onion salt: This is flavoured salt and is not the same as onion powder. If you have only the powder on hand, add the same quantity as the salt, but also add a pinch of regular salt to the recipe.

Plain flour: Do not substitute self-raising flour.

Potato powder: Dehydrated instant potato powder usually sold for making mashed potatoes. Sold in packets.

Quick-rise yeast: A dry yeast (granules) that acts faster than traditional dry yeast. Might also be referred to as "rapid rise yeast" on packaging. The yeast needs to be foamed before adding to recipes. Add all the yeast and the water it's foamed in to a recipe. Please see "Working with Yeast and Butter" in the "Organizing the Kitchen" chapter.

Skimmed milk powder: Sold in packets.

Souffle dish: A 15-cm diameter round white ceramic soufflé dish. It is used for baking small cakes. Sold in kitchenware shops. Several of the cake recipes can be made either in this dish or in a common 20-cm diameter metal tin.

Sweetened condensed milk: A thick, sweet milk sold in tins. Do not confuse with evaporated milk.

Unsalted butter: All recipes use unsalted butter. Unsalted margarine may be substituted, but results will vary slightly. For instance, biscuits will spread more during baking.

Unsweetened cocoa powder: Only use unsweetened cocoa as it will react differently in recipes than cocoa powder which is sweetened such as drinking chocolate. Contains no sugar. Please see "Measuring Ingredients" in the "Organizing the Kitchen" chapter.

MEASUREMENT ABBREVIATIONS

g = gram
L = litre
mL = millilitre
tsp = teaspoon
Tbsp = tablespoon

Bibliography

Bake It Yourself With Magic Baking Powder. Standard Brands Ltd., 1951.

Beard, James. *Beard on Bread*. Toronto: Random House Canada Ltd., 1983.

Malgieri, Nick. *Cookies Unlimited*. New York: HarperCollins, 2000.

The Velvet Touch. Robin Hood Flour Mills Ltd., undated vintage copy.

Weinstein, Bruce. *The Ultimate Candy Book*. New York: William Morrow, 2000.

Index